THE SHARPER WORD

THE SHARPER WORD

EDITED BY PAOLO HEWITT

Helter
Skelter
Publishing

London

This edition published in 1999 by Helter Skelter Publishing
4 Denmark Street, London WC2H 8LL

Cover design by by George Georgiou at General Practice,
photographed by Chris Clunn
Typesetting by Caroline Walker
Printed in Great Britain by Redwood Books, Trowbridge

A CIP record for this book is available from the British Library

ISBN 1-900924-10-2

CONTENTS

EDITOR'S INTRODUCTION

Little masterpieces, that's what they were. The jewels of the cities and the High Streets. Dressed with a stunning precision that spelt obsessive, a minefield of detail from head to toe, a work of art encased in Mohair and existing for clothes, music and kicks, Mods listened to the best music, danced the best dances and helped transform British cultural life.

They came from working class poor but consistently looked like a million pounds. Their lifestyle – crammed with exclusive records, serious dressing and obscure clubs – demanded money and total dedication. It was a tall order but Mods were unfazed. They aspired to greatness twenty-four hours a day, the first youth cult to do so.

What they hated in others – the tickets, the seven and sixers – is that they settled for so much less.

Modernism is Britain's most enduring lifestyle. Nearly forty years old now, still going strong. As befits a lifestyle that revolves around one hardened fact – attention to detail is absolute – Mod has no birthday. There is no one event, no one person, no item that you can point to and say, that's where the Holy Grail starts. Rather there is a just a jumble of social twists and cultural upheavals to guide us.

One of these is the day the second World War ended and Britain voted in a Labour Government, rejecting outright their wartime hero, the Conservative, Winston Churchill. This surprise victory for Labour leader Clement Attlee signalled the rejection of social inequality and the arrival of a new confidence within the working class. Their children would be its finest exemplars.

For the parents there would be no more doffing of the cap to the Lord of the Manor. Five years of living and dying together in fields of mud and blood had shattered the illusion that the upper classes were somehow better than everyone else. The working classes discovered their voice, their talents and as the country recovered from the war the seeds of a new optimism were sown. The sixties would be harvest time.

Attlee's Government didn't survive long but in 1953 Anthony Eden's Tory Government abolished compulsory National Service. That act alone assisted Mod's creation for it unwittingly created a difference between father and son. This split would further widen over the forthcoming years. The children would not settle for lives that were replicas of their parents. They would not think like them nor dress like them.

They – this brand new creation called the teenager – would strike out on its own, helped in its destiny by the changes blowing through every section of society. The parents of the teenager was a strong British economy. Unemployment in the late '50s was low. Money had started to circulate a lot more easily. Consequently, hire purchase – the buying of goods over a fixed period of time – was introduced. Now the working class could afford the luxury items they had once pined for like children with their faces mashed up against the sweet shop window. Material comforts would not be the sole preserve of the rich.

The trumpeter Donald Byrd argues that in every century cultural excellence starts at a low point but reaches its zenith around the mid mark before losing its impetus, its potency.

Maybe so, maybe not, but what can't be denied is that in the late '50s and early '60s, all of the art forms – music, film, literature, theatre, television – experienced immense shocks to the system.

They were overtaken by youth and injected with vigour and inventiveness. Traditional forms were challenged and overturned. The conditions for a new social outlook were being laid. Rightfully so. British pop culture was toothless, weak. The music of the time reflected its bankruptcy. There was no glamour, no sex, no rebels. There was Helen Shapiro. Matt Munro. There was mums and dad music. There was only light entertainment.

Mods were forced to take from different cultures because theirs was so utterly boring, so mind numbingly dreary and not suprisingly American fashion and music quickly caught their attention.

The Marshall Plan, in which America bankrolled several countries after the War, had established a link between the USA and the UK that is as strong today as it ever was. Many Mod fashions emanated from the States with Mods drawing heavily on the Brooks Brothers and casual preppy look that had been modelled by American Modernist jazz musicians. They adored these guys – the likes of Miles Davis – because they casually suggested – in their oh so hip manner and playing style – that there was so much more to music than either the trad jazz of their parents liking or the unbearably happy skiffle that was now sweeping the country.

These young jazzers with their insouciant manner, their publicised use of narcotics, the memorable celebration of their night-time lifestyle by America's Beat writers, their invention of a hip language, their cool demeanour, all of these hip characteristics suggested the existence of a secret society built on music and fashion and with no squares in sight.

It was all too wonderful. The Mods had to build their own model.

If skiffle had one use, it was its ability to encourage the young to form their own groups. A scene based around skiffle started in Soho's Old Compton Street when a club called The Two I's was opened. It was a place for the young by the young and serious social movers of the '60s – Andrew Loog Oldham for one – were to be found there, ordering endless cappuccinos from the owner's Gaggia machine, frustrated in the knowledge that the setting was correct but the music, this skiffle business, was so poor, so wrong.

The smarter brained of the set went out to improve matters. On their journey they discovered other American music, discovered the blues and the newly emerging r'n'b music that was firing up groups such as The Beatles. The pressure to provide public places to hear such music grew and grew. Such spaces were vital to the movement's development.

So when, for example, The Flamingo club in Wardour Street dropped its jazz policy and started playing r'n'b music Mod had another base to work from, somewhere – just like The Scene in Ham Yard – where Mods could congregate and dictate the fashion's direction.

But it wasn't just Stateside fashions and music that the Mods were attuned to. France and Italy were just as important for their clothes and films and books. (In this anthology Mod is tellingly described as a mix of 'John Lee Hooker, amphetamine and Jean Paul Sartre.') When Cecil Gee went on holiday in Italy and returned loaded down with bright coloured jumpers and tops, it meant one thing. The black and white world of post war Britain was about to explode into colour. The European lifestyle – a mix of intellectualism and casual living – was a magnet for Mods. They decided to ingratiate themselves as far as they could into this world.

Many Mods spent countless uncomprehending hours in the cinema watching non subtitled European movies. They might not have understood a word being said but they obsessively studied the characters' clothes and style and then adopted it for their own means.

They took the scooter from Italy and made it their own form of transport, a beautifully designed machine that was perfect for city travel. (Rockers tended to hail from the countryside and roared around on bulky, unwieldy machines.) They pretended to read foreign papers. They posed in cafés, smoked their cigarettes like Marcello Mastroianni.

The point about these longings, this urgent need for distinction, is that in the early '60s it took incredible dedication and hard work to realise them. Items, such as a Brooks Brothers shirt or a tailored Mohair suit were expensive and in many cases, not that easy to come by. Shops were not particularly stacked with the stuff. Mods simply reasoned that if you wanted something bad enough then you could get it. If you had a sharp mind and a determined soul then there was no excuse for slackness. It was a philosophy that was central to their outlook. Because proper Mods aspired to bettering themselves, to achieving absolute individualism, there would be animated discussions on the best way to wear your watch, how long the vent in your jacket should be, how many buttons were suitable.

They were dandies, aesthetes. For the first time young working class men were displaying an obsession with clothes that had only been previously noted in the gay movement. Oscar Wilde would have loved Mods. They transformed British menswear. Such factors – along with the re-emergence of American rock 'n' roll music which had briefly flowered in the late '50s but had now been castrated – amounted to the birth of pop culture, a process that was enormously strengthened by the success of The Beatles, who actually wrote their own songs and covered Motown and rock'n'roll songs.

But true Mods didn't like the Fab Four. Too popular (for which read obvious) but more importantly why listen to their r'n'b derived music when you could have the real thing? From a small obscure record shop. Hidden down some alleyway. Which you had to actively seek out. The same principle applied to the Rolling Stones and their appropriation of blues music. The original Mod was a purist and a snob but in a positive way. They said why settle for second best? Mods were so sure of themselves, so arrogant, they simply took no notice of you if you didn't see the world their way. They instinctively knew – no argument about it – that theirs was the best outlook. And that wasn't opinion. That was a fact of life.

Another fact is that Mods – in keeping with society's technological developments and sense of growing aspirations of the '60s, (this was after all the jet age) – wanted a better life than anything previously experienced by their parents. Most Mods left school at 15. One because school treated them with utter contempt and taught them nothing of value and two, because they needed the money their lifestyle demanded.

As Mod's recruits were mainly drawn from the working class they were determined to use everything in their power to avoid the factory lines they had been groomed for. They had seen the best minds of their parents destroyed by the mind freezing and dull work that factory lines demanded, and Mods would take no part in such brain washing.

As the economy grew, Mods found themselves infiltrating sharp jobs in advertising or film, work that had previously been denied them. They became office boys, spent their days smug in the knowledge that they were not only much better dressed than their bosses but one day, one fine day, they would take his job and run the show themselves.

Mods were ambitious and selfish little creatures. You have to be when you want the best from life. Then, at weekends, they submerged themselves in their secret world of clubs and music and drugs and buying clothes. They never slept, just pumped themselves up with amphetamine. Friday night began watching Cathy McGowan introduce the TV show *Ready Steady Go* and then everything literally sped up as the weekend flashed by in a blur of pills and caffeine until suddenly it was Sunday night and time to wind down.

Amphetamine was the right drug for Mods. It gave them confidence, awareness and inspiration. It allowed them to dance all night, to perfect their moves. But it also provided a fearsome comedown and some Mods never quite recovered from their intake.

When the best Mods went to clubs they never did anything so crass as spend all their time inside the place. They often stood outside, showing off their clothes, creating statements, devising missions. Girls were a part of it but in the top Mod clubs the art of pulling was never really an option. Why waste the energy when it could be better spent dancing to perfection to the sound of such sweet sweet soul music?

Mods were Mohair radicals and they excelled in race relations. Unlike the rockers – who had been stupid enough to swallow the virulent Moseley propaganda directed against the West Indians citizens and picked fights with them in Nottingham and Notting Hill – the Mods welcomed the Caribbeans with open arms. For they brought with them life, excitement, glamour, clothes, music, a 24 hour lifestyle. Mods instinctively knew that this culture would play a huge part in reshaping Britain. And they were right. For me this is their greatest achievement and something they have never been given true credit for.

In the sixties the single reigned supreme, a time when your life could really be changed by just one song, one 45 blaring from your transistor radio. All the great singles of this time were designed in a Mod style. That is they announced themselves, made their point with real style and then quit before they got boring. They were well dressed tunes with neat arrangements and smart twists to endear them to the teen listener. All I have to say is, 'Waterloo Sunset" by The Kinks. Yet Mods had little to do with pop music. R'n'b was their bag. So although The Small Faces, The Creation, The Action and a hundred others emerged with bouffants and basket weave shoes, boasting great singers like Steve Marriott or Reggie King, the proper Mods, the inner circle, were never that excited about them. Their heroes were Stax artists, Motown musicians. Out of all the white performers in circulation, very, very few performers – Georgie Fame was one – got the nod.

Soon, though, it didn't matter who had the goods or not because in 1964, original Modernism was dead. 1964 was the first year of Bank Holiday weekend fights with small groups of rockers and of tabloids reporting the Mod lifestyle on their front pages, exposing their world to the squares. The cognoscenti were disgusted. It was all so shameful.

The true Mod wanted out. Popularity had totally diluted his cause and the Mods now saw how an elite movement can not sustain itself once it attracts huge numbers. Fighting on a beach! Scuffing your shoes and ruining your trousers. It was all so…wrong, horribly, horribly wrong.

Proper Mods did one of two things. They either settled down and conducted the rest of their lives with the kind of style and grace we had come to expect of them. Or they discovered the new Mary Jane, LSD, grew hair and moustaches and started listening to Jimi Hendrix. End of story? No. Modernism continued but in different forms, different guises. But that's a different story for another time.

Modernism dictated the first half of that amazing decade, the '60s. For those of us too young to have experienced this time – we tantalisingly passed through it as wide eyed bambinos – this period in British society will always exert a huge fascination for us.

Modernism was in at the start of British pop culture. The young dedicated masterpieces whose history has been hitherto not accorded the attention they deserve made a massive contribution to our culture. Theirs was a youth of sharp kicks, of accepting all kinds of cultures to mould their own code of conduct, a creation of ideas that still powerfully resonate today. Mods were the first to take something and then customise it for their own means

They were the first to dedicate their lives twenty four hours a day to the cause and yet Mods have never been given any decent press or afforded their rightful place in history. I suspect that's because the media world remains suspicious of clothes, which stems from the '70s rock culture they were raised in. One of its unstated rules was that if you dressed to impress, there was something mistrustful about you, something frivolous. And those who did dress to impress tended to frighten these media types. 'They remind me of school bullies,' one *NME* writer said of Oasis.

'Modernism is just about shopping,' sneered the *NME* editor recently. Yeah, like Punk is just about wearing a safety pin. Such statements capture perfectly the contempt that many writer folk have for anyone using clothes as a statement in conjunction with their art. (See Rowland, Kevin, reaction to.) But Modernism shrugs off all attacks because put simply, it just doesn't care too much about these people and their world. Modernism searches for truth. That's why it's Britain's longest standing youth cult. It has survived and prospered because it is built on a set of principles that remain firm.

Modernism has longevity because it recognises two absolute facts. True style and quality never ever dates and that as long as there's a money-go-round, there will always be someone wanting to dress up to fuck off a world that constantly wants to put you down.

Paolo Hewitt, Autumn, '98

This anthology concerns itself with the young Mod's forgotten history. It aims, through the work of others, to unravel Modernism, to give the reader a sense of some of its mysteries and splendour. I have drawn on many literary forms – fiction, journalism, unpublished writings – in the hope that these collected pieces form a satisfying whole. The focus is mainly on the '60s because this is when the young Mod's story begins and ends and because this really was the time when Modernism was about, in Pete Meaden's choice quote, 'clean living under difficult circumstances.' P.H.

CREDITS

Thanks to Sean Body at Helter Skelter whose excellent idea this book was. Applause also for Mike O'Connell with his help in securing many of the books. Many thanks to Tasha Lee and the Heavenly crew for use of their photo copier and to Michelle Potter and the Solid Bond outfit for a similar favour.

This book's cover was designed by George Georgiou at General Practice (0171 383 7992) photographed by Chris Clunn (0171 404 9646) and the target was supplied by Lush Productions (0171 486 1990). Front cover girl, Sahika Arif, the sweetest thing this side of heaven productions.

THIS BOOK IS DEDICATED TO JEFF BARRETT, THE NOW MODERNIST,
AND HIS FAMILY, AND TO THE BEAUTIFUL MEMORY OF
PETE MEADEN, 1942-1978

1 YELLOW SOCKS ARE OUT – NIK COHN

One of the greatest ever pop writers, blessed with style and a telling use of detail, sets the scene as clothes now take on new meanings for men.

The first time that I came to London, in 1956, I used to spend all my afternoons in the Charing Cross Road, with my nose pressed up tight against the musicians' window at Cecil Gee. Inside, there was a Vathek-like magnificence, the most splendorous sights that I'd seen in my life: danceband uniforms of lamé or silk or satin, all tinselled and starred, a shimmering mass of maroons and golds and purples, silvers and pure sky-blues, like fireworks.

It was one of London's great landmarks and, to me, the finest of all Gee's creations. For Mister Swish himself, however, it must have been a backwater, one tiny facet of an empire that had grown to fourteen shops by 1959 and had reached a yearly turnover of almost £2 million.

Right up to 1957, he remained unchallenged, both in theatricality and value. Whatever the fashion, he did it first and did it brashest and, when rock 'n' roll came in, he dressed Tommy Steele and Marty Wilde, just as he had once dressed Jack Hylton.

He also had a near-monopoly of modern jazzmen, who wished to look American. By the fifties, the transatlantic style no longer meant zoot suits or hand-painted ties. Instead, this was the age of Cool, of Gerry Mulligan and Chet Baker, and drummers with hooded eyes and a cigarette hanging off their lower lips, short-cropped Nero haircuts, hypodermics and shades. Everything was saturnine, understated, and the suits were dark and conservative but cut bigger and more butch than most English suits, with lots of chest and shoulder.

If you wanted to get it exactly right, you had to go to Ben Harris, a Soho tailor, who cut the most advanced and authentic-looking American suits in London ('Almost a genius,' says Eric Joy, who worked for him, 'and the best, most honest man I've met'); but if you were poor and impatient, which most musicians were, you made a compromise with Cecil Gee and consoled your-self with Old Spice aftershave, which was then unavailable in England and had to be brought back from New York by Geraldo's navy.*

The modernist look was used not only by musicians themselves but by the whole Bop scene, semi-pros and fans and hangers-on, and by many of the younger West End hustlers.

Still, this was all on a very small scale compared to the Italian Look, which Gee launched in 1956.

'After I opened up in Shaftesbury Avenue, I knew there had to be a return to neatness, after the razzle-dazzle American styles,' he says. 'Then I went to Italy for my holidays. There were all these marvellous fabrics and colours, and the manufacturers would give you anything you asked for, and I thought *This is for me*. So I put on a whole Italian season and that was the first time that elegance came to England.'

Actually, there was less divine inspiration involved than this might suggest. The San Remo festivals, and the work of designers like Brioni, had already made Italian styles known over here, at least within the trade, and fashion journalists had been predicting a boom for months. Cecil Gee did not discover the look; he was merely the first with courage and energy enough to get behind it and shove.

Brioni, of Rome, was the leading Italian stylist at the time and Gee's look was a variation and tarting-up of his basic shape: a short, box-like jacket, with narrow trousers in a lightweight fabric like mohair.

Even in Brioni's version, this produced an effect of squatness and constriction; but when Gee took it up and exaggerated it one came to look like a man in his kid brother's clothes. The jacket would ride up at the back, thereby giving the style its nickname

* Geraldo, the band leader, supplied musicians to the transatlantic liners and throughout the fifties, they provided an invaluable source of supply for all things American.

the 'bum-freezer', and the pants were too short in the ankle, and the buttons too tight across the chest. Worn with pointed-toe shoes, which pinched the feet, the result was one of agonized, bottled-up confinement and every time one sneezed, a button popped.

The look had many refinements. As well as its shortness, the jacket had narrow lapels and a rounded, scooped-out hem. The shirts were small-collared and, by the late fifties, button-down. The ties were skinny. Hair was worn short. Everything was skimped – narrow legs, pointed feet, no shoulders.

It was not elegant, no matter what Gee had intended. Aesthetically, it was no great improvement on the High Street, the dark grey undead. But at least it was action – it was new, and a bit flashy, and it became the basic young man's suit of the late '50s, especially in London and the south. In fact, it was an even greater success than the Teddy Boy look. It wasn't exclusively working-class; it had no delinquent undertones; it was almost respectable. Hard-line Teds would have nothing to do with it, thinking it soft.

More than any previous style, it was classless, not worn by extremists but by jog-along youths in the span from working to middle class, boys with jobs and families and fiancées, boys who carried no razors and didn't swear in front of ladies.

Furthermore, it lasted. Over the next eight years there was a whole sequence of similar styles, all based on short jackets and narrow pants: first the Italian Look itself; then the round-collared Cardin suit, later revived as the Beatle suit; and finally the Mod suit, the first standby of Carnaby Street. Elsewhere, it survived even longer. In black Africa, bum-freezers and pointed-toe shoes are still going strong today. 'You'd be surprised,' says Don McCullin, who has photographed innumerable African wars. 'The number of times I've come up over a sandhill and seen a pair of winklepickers, pointing up at the sky.'

Only two minorities refused to tag along: ton-up boys, later to be Rockers, and Beatniks.

Ton-up boys were the natural successors to Teds, in attitude, language and values. Only their uniform was changed. Instead of mock-Edwardiana, they took their style from Marlon Brando's film *The Wild Ones*, and from the Hell's Angels who lay behind it, and they wore black leather jackets, with studding on the back, and high black boots. They rode on motorbikes and travelled in packs, and lived off greasy eggs and chips, and hung out in transport cafés, and liked blondes with big breasts, and still worshipped Elvis Presley.

In the late fifties, a firm called Anello & Davide, who made theatrical boots in the Charing Cross Road, began to promote the Cuban-heeled, or Chelsea boot and that became part of the uniform as well.

It was a beautiful, ornate and decadent object, elastic-sided with built-up heels, maybe two inches high, which gave it a deeply hollowed instep. It spoke of heroics, of gunfights in the noonday sun, of violence and sex together – and ton-up boys, who saw themselves as desperadoes, loved it. Not only ton-up boys, either – less stylized groups took it up as well, kids without motorbikes. Soon it had spread throughout the whole spectrum of teenage hooliganism and flash. Then the multiple shoestores adopted it and made it almost respectable. They gave it a winklepicker toe and lost the depth of the instep, which was its great splendour, and the Chelsea boot became part of the standard blue jeans and hair-oil uniform, specially in the North.

At the same time, the first Beats were emerging. They were purely an American imitation, gleaned from Jack Kerouac and Allen Ginsberg, and most of them were concentrated in London, although each provincial town would have its own cell, maybe twenty beards strong, huddled together in basements, where they listened to poetry and jazz and looked solemn.

In the bohemian tradition, they wore anti-dress: long hair, rancid old sweaters and paint-stained jeans, bare feet or sandals, and Ban the Bomb badges. They wished for profundity and originality and sometimes, rather nervously, because they weren't used to it, they would pass a joint around.

For themselves, they didn't matter much. In America, the movement grew quite large and meant something, paved the way for real changes; but in England, there were never more than a couple of thousand full-timers and they were always a bit of a joke, tame fall-guys for cartoonists.

Their influence, however, was considerable. In the long term they proved to be forerunners, advance warnings of the Hippies to come, in their long hair and beards, their total contempt for straight society, their conformity within anarchy.

In the short term, they also provided a base for hordes of part-timers, who took the high seriousness of the Beat stance and turned it into games. A generation of art students, and those who hoped to be taken for art students, and rebellious sixth-formers, and Aldermaston marchers in general joined in the pretence. They grew their hair a bit long and produced paint-stains for their jeans and mouthed a few slogans about squares and warmongers. But instead of studying Zen Buddhism and immersing themselves in Thelonious Monk, they settled for getting drunk and jumping up and down to Trad.

They wore impossibly baggy sweaters and, often, battered bowler hats with Acker written on them, after Acker Bilk, the clarinettist. They went on marches, as much for the sex as the politics and, altogether, had a jolly good time.

University students, meanwhile, tended more towards the duffel coat, which was also anti-dress, but tacitly so. It had first become popular in the army surplus days after the war and then, in 1951, had been brought out commercially, for the use of 'gentlemen, gentleman farmers, mariners, men of leisure and intellectuals'.

At first, they lived up to this and Winston Churchill bought one for his birthday, complete with fur collar. But gradually they became a uniform for students and readers of *The Outsider*. With their hoods and toggles and utter shapelessness, they were at least defiant in their ugliness. They weren't a gesture like bohemian anti-dress, aimed at whipping up rage and horror; rather they were a quittance, a denial of all interest, to be worn with curry stains down the front and the poems of Rimbaud in the pocket, so saying I am above vanity, above flesh; I move in higher regions.

All the time, however so gradually that you couldn't really put your finger on what was happening, the level of general male interest in clothes was rising. There might be nothing as radical as the Teds; but the industry as a whole was beginning to stir.

Everything was loosening. As sexual and social standards became more flexible, and England settled into Wondermac cosiness, it was inevitable that dress became more permissive as well.

The old strictures hardly applied any more. It wasn't necessary for clothes to announce one's parentage, nor that they should stay the same for ever.

This last was the biggest shift – the speed with which styles changed. Before the war, any new fashion had been good for a decade at least; now it might disappear within months.

So it was, when George Melly went to Cecil Gee and asked for a pair of yellow socks, that the salesman stared at him and smirked. 'Oh no, sir,' he said. 'Yellow socks are out,' and Melly went away blushing.

In and Out: it was a new concept, and fascinating. From then on, Carnaby Street was inevitable.

2

"The big difference between the trad jazz people and the modern jazz people, which is where the word 'mod' really comes from – the modernists who went to modern jazz gigs – was that the mod thing tended to be more working class or East End Jewish, whereas the trad thing tended to be public school dropouts – much more English, people leaping up and down to trad jazz, already the thing of being ostentatious in dress, whereas the modernist thing was very much not ostentatious. Somebody else might notice how you had your tie, someone who knew about things like that, but it wasn't ostentatious. But we did want to function as a parallel world."

Robert Wyatt, in Jonathan Green's Days In The Life.

3   MODS – RICHARD BARNES

Barnes' book Mods *is quite simply the bible so far as books on Modernism go. Richard Barnes was there and what's more remembered it all.*

It was from their Modern Jazz tastes that they named themselves. They called themselves Modernists.

There were still only a handful but they were noticed and talked about and their clothes copied by others. They would gravitate towards the West End. 'They'd sit around in coffee bars like the Bastille,' said Ric. 'They'd meet up with other guys like themselves and sit and admire each other.'

Slowly their influence spread. Their outlook on things affected other kids who would aspire to be like them. Gradually the Modernists became a minor cult.

The Italian look went through many modifications. Mostly they were just changes of detail and very slight, but a definite direction was emerging.

Most suits were still bought made to measure. So each time one was made it was slightly different to suit each individual. For instance, they had rounded jacket fronts. Two, three or four button jackets. Covered buttons. The box jacket could have small side vents, 1", 2" or 3" long, or a half belt at the back, or both. Cuffs could be open, with or without a link button or a butterfly cuff, which is an open cuff coming to a point. Some jackets were very cut-away and rounded to look like a bolero.

Trousers were narrow but varied between 14" to 17" bottoms. There was a brief period of bell bottoms. Then came slanted bottoms, or even stepped bottoms where the trouser leg bottoms were cut at the seams so that the back was lower than the front by about an inch. Trouser legs were also finished with a small slit in the side seam at the bottom, usually anything up to 3" long. There could be little details like small buttons sewn on the seams of trousers just above the shoes. Suits were still predominantly blue and dark blue or road strong black and blue stripes. Also another popular fabric then was Prince of Wales check.

The shirts which at first had a short pointed collar gave way to long pointed collars with a very close gap at the front. This made ties a lot slimmer and the knot smaller. Narrow knitted ties were the favourite.

Shoes were often made to measure, preferably at Stans of Battersea. This was expensive but was the only way the kids could get what they wanted. The extended point shoe, nicknamed the winklepicker, was still in fashion. The points were often 3" or 4" long. Sometimes they were made with a Cuban heel. Buckles on shoes and side laces came in. Imitation crocodile sides, known as 'mock Crock' was a big thing for shoes.

It was also very smart to wear shoes of red or green leather. Casual clothes like cardigans and 'Fred Perrys' started appearing. A 'Fred Perry' was a knitted cotton short-sleeved sports shirt with a three-button opening at the top. It was really designed as tennis wear. Fred Perry who presumably designed it, had been a famous tennis player. There were cheaper versions but it was better to be seen in the genuine article with the little laurel wreath emblem embroidered on the left breast. It was a very versatile and distinctively Mod item, and could be worn with Levis or a suit. It still looked smart to wear a suit without a tie, if you wore a Fred Perry shirt, and this look lasted with one or two modifications (mainly to the suits) throughout the whole Mod era.

Italian hair cuts had come in in about 1960. Not all barbers could do an Italian haircut as most of them still simply cut men's hair rather than styling it, but for about 6/- (as opposed to the normal 2/6d) you could get the 'Perry Como' cut. The style had a different, 'dry look' because kids had no oil or grease on it and in those days it wasn't easy to get out of the barber's without him rubbing some sort of oil into your hair.

After this came the 'College Boy' cut, which was shorter than the 'Perry Como', and then the 'French Crop', which was like a crew cut but longer — about two inches all over. Another new hairstyle was the 'The Crop', which was like a grown out 'College Boy' with a higher parting. All these styles were short, neat and clean-looking — the distinguishing feature of the earliest Mods.

As early as 1959 there were kids with motor scooters and by 1960 there were little gangs known as 'Scooter Boys'. They too were very clothes conscious: a forerunner of the later scooter Mod look. They wore Parkas, ex-army khaki-coloured all-weather cape-sized coats which they could wear over their outer clothes. They wore them for practical reasons more than for their looks, although later Parkas became fashionable.

Levi jeans caught on about that time. They cost about 42/6d. They were all button fly fronted and stiff as cardboard when you first wore them. Kids had to sit in the bath and shrink them on. They used to scrub and then later bleach them to get a faded look, the more bleached-looking the better.

The changes in life that were taking place in the late fifties and early sixties were cleverly summed up by Lionel Bart in his song, 'Fings Ain't What They Used To Be'. Local family grocers were being replaced by Supermarkets. 'Frothy' Coffee Bars and Wimpy bars appeared. 24-hour launderettes took over from laundries, bagwash and municipal wash-houses. It was all part of an Americanisation that was taking place. Modernists identified with all these new 'convenient' innovations. They thought England still too fuddy-duddy and conservative. They were the generation of advertising and soft sell. The advertising industry had been Americanised too since the introduction of commercial television. Modernists really wanted to own that E-type Jag and have that blonde hanging on their arm.

They also looked to the Continent for fashion inspiration. They'd see French students and tourists in the summer who were much better dressed than themselves. So they went to French clubs in London. The most popular were ones catering for French students, La Poubelle and Le Kilt. Willie Deasey from East London regularly visited these two clubs. 'The clothes the French guys wore were so well-cut. We weren't used to good casual clothes. They had hipster trousers and round-toed shoes, beautiful shoes. They had well-cut suits made from lightweight fabrics. The stuff used to look good for dancing. We used to get all our ideas for clothes from them.'

They immersed themselves in all things French. 'We used to go to see French movies as much as we could,' remembers

Johnny Moke, a friend of Willie Deasey's. 'Mostly I couldn't understand a bloody word of it. Next day I'd tell everybody, "I say, I saw a great French film, you should go and see it, it's absolutely wonderful." I went to see a film called *YoYo*. I sat through about an hour of it and said to my girlfriend, "He's not talking." Afterwards she explained that the star, Marcel Marceau, never talked anyway, he just mimed. I didn't realise, you know, just 'cos it was French I was sitting there.'

Another of Willie and Johnny's friends took it all a bit too seriously. 'We never smoked but would light up a Gauloise just to be seen with it. We all got into the French films and magazines, but Les went berserk. He used to wear a striped jumper and a beret and eat garlic and everything. He started to learn French. We saw him once sitting in Aldgate Wimpy holding up a copy of *Le Soir*. When we went in and joined him we saw that he was really reading the *Sunday Pictorial* which he had concealed in between the middle pages. It was all a pose. There was even a time when we saw him walking along wearing his beret and striped jumper and carrying a loaf of French bread under his arm'.

Of course, Modernists had Continental heroes. There weren't many English stars that they admired, apart from perhaps Sean Connery's James Bond, but they were fans of people like Marcello Mastroianni and Juliette Greco.

Although a Mod look had emerged there was still no sense of common identity that embraced the whole movement. This was probably because Mods existed mostly in clubs and coffee bars and in each others houses. The press hadn't yet 'discovered' them.

They were still very localized. Each area would have its fashion purist as leader and he would influence the kids in his area. They'd see him and his friends in the dance hall or club and copy his clothes, while he in his turn would meet other 'faces' in clubs and coffee bars in the West End and take note of what was being worn by whom. So within the general attitude to clothes and living that had emerged, there were different pockets of kids with different local variations.

Then in 1962, *Town* magazine printed photographs and an interview with some 'faces' from Stamford Hill. One of these was 15-year-old Mark Feld (who later became Mark Bolan and a successful seventies pop star). They talked of their attitude to clothes and bemoaned the difficulty of finding good tailors. 'Bilgorri of Bishopsgate – he's a great tailor … All the faces go to Bilgorri. And John Stephens. He's very good on trousers.' They also spoke of finding cheaper clothes suits from Burtons and shirts costing 14/6d from C&A. 'Some faces won't look at them because they're only 14/6d. That's just ridiculous,' Mark Feld said, and told of a gingham shirt he'd seen that morning in Woolworths, 'Only ten bob; a few alterations and it would look as good as a four guinea job from John Michael.'

The *Town* magazine article was the first media coverage of these young devotees of fashion, and it was inspiration and confirmation for all the others. It was in 1962 that all the individual and diverse elements finally fused into the overall Mod style. It was still very male-dominated and largely centred around the London suburbs and the Home Counties, but was gradually spreading out.

It was now important to walk properly, hold a cigarette the correct way and know the right way even to stand. Correct stance was important because a lot of time was spent hanging around posing and talking and showing oneself off. Johnny Moke remembers, 'You'd have to look totally relaxed, but right. You'd have to pose, so you sort of slouched, you put your leg against the wall. To look cool, you'd put your hands in your Levi's or your jacket pocket with your thumbs sticking out.' Rik from Wembley remembers that stance was important. 'Feet had to be right. If you put your hand in your trouser pocket, you never pulled the jacket up so it was wrinkled. You'd have the top button done up and the jacket would be pulled back behind the arm so that you didn't ruin the line. You'd only ever put one hand in your pocket if you were wearing a jacket. It was a bit foppish, but quite subtle.'

There was still difficulty in finding the right kind of clothes. Suits would be made to measure and in London there were shops like John Michael which stocked fairly reasonable stuff, but the real discovery for most kids was His Clothes in Carnaby Street. It's different for anyone who wasn't around then to imagine how revolutionary Carnaby Street was, especially if you see what it has descended to these days.

I first went there with Pete Townshend. Somebody had told us about the street and one day while we were in the West End we decided to have a look. We couldn't find it at first, it really was a back-street of London. It wasn't a very attractive street either. One side had a huge windowless brick-built warehouse owned by the Electricity Board or someone. There were four, or maybe five, men's clothes shops and a tobacconist's. I can't remember much else and I don't think there was much else. There was more than one shop called His Clothes, then, I think, Paul's and Domino Male and Donis. This day was wet and grey and the street was deserted. But when we saw the clothes we couldn't believe them. It was the more colourful clothes that amazed me – I mean, candy-pink denim hipsters for men? Fantastic. Outrageous.

In most men's outfitters at that time you'd see lines of jackets or trousers or something and they'd all look the same. Some were black, some were dark black, others were jet black and if you wanted to be a little extrovert you could risk a black one with, wait for it, a grey speckle running through it. But in His Clothes not only were there fantastic daring colours, but there were loads of different styles and fabrics. All of this was crammed into a little space with lots of good music coming from speakers on the wall. You could try things on and handle what you liked without any besuited salesman 'advising' you. The assistants were all very young and friendly and polite. As was John Stephen himself. He called everybody 'Sir' and went to a lot of trouble to be helpful.

There was a sense of excitement in Carnaby Street. It wasn't very well known then but was doing well, and had a growing clientèle. I think most of its trade was on Saturdays, since, as I said, it was deserted this particular weekday. The only other person we saw was a tall, well-dressed young negro who bought a pair of the coloured denim hipster trousers This negro was obviously homosexual and I realised that homosexuals had been buying that stuff for years. They were the only people with the nerve to wear it, but in the early sixties the climate of opinion was changing, the Mods were wearing the more effeminate and colourful clothes of Carnaby Street. John Stephen stated simply that he thought men 'should be able to wear whatever they liked'.

4   HISTORY – IRISH JACK

Irish Jack was a very early supporter of The Who and was also rumoured to be the Mod that Townshend's later project, Quadrophenia *was based upon. Here we are privy to his unpublished essay concerning his discovery of Modernism.*

I know where the Mods started. I mean, I know but I don't know who the first mod was. I'd personally like to shake his hand though because becoming a mod changed me completely into a different person. It was like being reborn in a way. One minute we were just ordinary blokes in the Goldhawk – the next thing you know we were all bleedin' Mods. It seemed to happen overnight. Like somebody switched on an electric current. I owe a lot to that geezer the first Mod whoever he is, cos I think I might have seen him! I can remember walking down King Street in Hammersmith on a balmy summer's evening 1963. In the distance I heard the distinct piston pop of an Italian scooter. That neat little sound. When I turned around I saw this geezer on a brand new silver Chromed Vespa GS. He had a stack of tiny spot lamps mounted on the front and half a dozen mirrors. Behind him a ten foot aerial dipped into the wind and fitted to the top was a very classy fox tail. Dead keen, the whole thing was. The bloke on the scooter was wearing a pair of American sneakers with an army parka coat over a suit. He looked brilliant, with cropped hair parted in the middle like he was French. I just stood and stared in disbelief at the sight of this 'cos in all honesty the scooter resembled a Ragman chariot. it was a breathtaking moment for me and a pretty decisive one. I would have given anything to have looked as good as that bloke did that night. The first Mod!

Next day I told my friend Tommy Shelley about what I'd seen. He just smiled quietly like he'd heard about it already or even seen the bloke. We agreed to meet up Saturday afternoon in Philip Grant's shop in King Street. When we got there the shop was jammed with geezers from Hammersmith and Acton buying up Fred Perrys and sta-prest trousers. Suddenly it was everywhere. The most unstoppable period of my life. Another mate of mine, Martin Gaish, went and nicked a pair of Hush Puppies from Lilley & Skinner – but I had to pay for mine. Gaish could nick anything really cos his hands were like greased lightning. They wouldn't let him into Woolworths.

I have to admit that my uncle & aunt weren't exactly over the moon about the blue plastic mac I bought. I wore it belted down tight in the middle with a double knot. And neither were they too crazy about my cousin Janice's college scarf draped over my shoulder. But how could I explain to them that was the way every geezer in west London was dressing up? It still didn't matter; my uncle reckoned I looked like an Italian pimp. I went and looked in the bedroom mirror to check this out. He was wrong. I looked cool. A dangerous man. A mannish boy.

When the fashion really began to take off it took any one of us seven or eight weeks to save for a bit of gear that was old hat after a month. That's how much we cared about how we looked. Mods hated finding themselves out of sync with leading faces. We were like an organised army really. We were everywhere. I mean, there were Mods in Burnley and Bolton and probably even Glenda Loch but London really was the place, London had Soho; no one else did. Leading faces appeared in fashion magazines and classy stuff like *Town* wearing Levi's faded to perfection and Henley boating jackets. Lambrettas and Vespas – the road to the coast for pills and good music. See, us Mods, we were the only ones that really cared about how we looked. And judging by the speed of the fashion, it soon became apparent that the only way any Mod worth his salt could keep abreast of things was to have a job. We were the only youth culture that honestly believed in work. Teds and Beatniks didn't. We had to work to earn the money to buy the clothes. I mean, I was a bleedin' filing clerk with the L.E.B. and my friend was a meat pie packer – and we were just as Mod as each other. That was the thing about this big army of Mods we could be working at anything really and still dress smart and be Mod.

The first time I heard the expression "Up west" I hadn't a clue what it meant. I thought it was a dog at the White City. But soon every Mod in London was using the expression. "Up west" meant being up the West End, the Soho district of London. When you were up west with Mods from all over London and the sticks you couldn't help but feel theatrical, for west see, was where all the leading plays were and where you could see a film before it went out on General Release. There was a prescribed air of exclusiveness about the place that seemed to fit the Mod ethic to a tee. Wardour Street and Gerrard Street were the main arteries where hundreds of Mods gathered to pose and score pills on Friday and Saturday nights – but mostly Saturday nights after the suburban pubs and clubs closed.

I used to get the Tube from Goldhawk Road to Hammersmith, walk under the subway and catch the Piccadilly Line to Piccadilly Circus. When I'd come up the steps of Piccadilly it actually had the sensation of coming up out of the ground like a great Phoenix. Suddenly I'd dramatically appear. You came up out of the ground and instantly you were surrounded by a tidal wave of people. A fucking World party if you like. Everyone. Mods; young boys and girls pilled to the eyeballs. News vendors with dirty magazines hidden under the counter. Drug pushers; sixpence each for French Blues, a shilling for a Roaring Twenty. Prostitutes; ten quid for it, a fiver for a hand job. 'End of the world' placard bearers. Coppers looking for a collar. Country bumpkins up town for the day. And tourists; fucking thousands of tourists. No wonder I felt like an ace face as I strutted along Shaftesbury Avenue like a well plumed peacock with my hands buried deep in my jacket pockets. Bloody cool, that was. That was the thing about being up west on a Saturday night: in one sense you were nobody; just another one of Soho's lost souls – but at the same time, you're standing at the pedestrian crossing in the middle of a mob of camera clicking tourists and you're there. Bloody Mod from head to toe. And you're so cool you could be Albert Finney or Tom Courtenay – just nipped out of the Garrick for a breather.

The ace face in everyone's book was a geezer called Peter Meaden. A nervous wreck. He spoke at you at about a hundred miles an hour and used to sound like an American DJ. He was really as Cockney as Bow Bells but usually pills made him sound American. He was like a king. Well, he was king Mod, that was for sure. He was plugged into everything and lived his life a word, a style, a dance step ahead of us all. He lived in cramped surroundings in a ten by eight room in Monmouth Street, which of course was London W1 and a very flash address to give anyone. All he ever had to his name – apart from the gift of the gab – was a mattress, an electric kettle, a record player, a filing cabinet and an ironing board. Those were the ingredients of who he was.

When I heard that this guy Meaden had become the manager of The Who it sounded like a marriage made in heaven. They were perfect for each other, Meaden and The Who. A couple of weeks after he took over the band he changed their name to The High Numbers and told all the Mods in the Goldhawk Club to stop calling them The Who. We did. Because we believed in this bloke Meaden. I still reckoned The Who was a much better name though.

One night, he told me The High Numbers were going to release their first ever single, a song called 'I'm The Face'. It sounded like a great title for a song and I asked Meaden if Townshend had written it. He said no and refused to say any more on the subject. The next week I went down the Goldhawk Club. Meaden had a little sales table set up under the stage selling copies of 'I'm The Face'. I didn't buy one cos I knew I'd get a free copy from my friend Townshend. Meaden approached me later in the bar and said if I was willing to take some copies of the record down Shepherd's Bush market the next day (Saturdays) I could earn myself a nice little commission. I took one dozen records from him and got so excited about selling copies of 'I'm The Face', I actually forgot to ask how much the commission was.

Saturday afternoon I went off down Shepherd's Bush Market thinking I'd shift all twelve copies within the hour – what a fool I was. The market was jammed as usual with bargain hunters, Mod girls buyin' summer slingbacks and West Indians haggling over the price of carpets and crockery. There was also the overhanging smell of bird seed. I spent the next three hours baking in the hot July sun and standing in the middle of the walk-through handing out copies of 'I'm The Face'. Nobody wanted to know. Ever felt like a leper? In the entire three hours I managed to sell just three copies and in the end I got so fed up of people ignoring me and this great bloody band I believed in so much, I said; 'Sod this, I'm off home.' When I got indoors I stepped into a lukewarm bath and it felt like heaven.

I bumped into Peter Meaden at the Goldhawk Club later that night and he told me he had spent the whole day running around trying to get record shops to take 'I'm The Face'. I know I'd felt pretty exhausted after my stint in the market but Meaden looked absolutely fucked. He told me he'd been everywhere. I told him I had only managed to sell three copies of the record and he looked very disappointed. Then his face completely dropped when I said I'd left the nine unsold copies at home. Meaden, very begrudgingly, handed over my commission. I took the little brown envelope from him – it was the standard pay envelope like at work – and when I opened it up I discovered that Meaden was paying out his commission not in money but in pills!

'I'm The Face' never got anywhere. The record company Fontana only pressed about a thousand and anyway they had no real interest in The High Numbers. Someone said Meaden gave away a stack of records to disc jockeys who never kept their word, and I think the bass player John Johns or Johnny Allison or John Browne, or whatever John Entwistle was calling himself at the time: his aunt bought about a dozen copies and completely dried up the stock in an Acton record shop.

I never gave Peter Meaden his nine unsold records back and I don't think we were ever quite the same after that. See, what actually happened is this: my aunt Carol was always nagging me about keeping my room tidy. So whenever I heard her approach with her favourite feather duster, I used to scoop up everything off the bed and keep it out of sight. My uncle John kept this old piano in my room and that was usually the most likely dumping place for High Numbers literature and unsold copies of 'I'm The Face'. Usually when the coast was clear I'd reach into the back of the piano and fish out most of what I'd dumped. Sometimes not everything would be retrieved and that's where a load of – nowadays pretty valuable – High Numbers pamphlets and nine unsold copies of 'I'm The Face' are sunk.

Only I always intended on clearing everything out and of course I got home one day to discover a big space in my room where the piano used to be. My aunt informed me that my uncle had at long last donated it to a rag and bone man who happened to call and I was almost in tears. Jesus Christ! Imagine it: nine copies of The High Numbers' 'I'm The Face' stuffed down the back of an old piano and my uncle gets rid of it. One copy of the record is probably worth ten times more nowadays than what he got for the piano.

5 CARNABY STREET – NIK COHN

Cohn again. I wasn't too interested in Carnaby Street per se but I wanted something on John Stephens, the Glaswegian who transformed London shopping. This is the best account of him although I do hear a biography is on the way.

What was different, straightaway, was the scale. Bill Green, basically, had thought in terms of a single successful, gossip-column boutique; John Stephen intended a holocaust. From the word go, he meant to turn menswear upside down, change everything. 'My ambition is simple,' he told *Men's Wear*, when he was just beginning to expand. 'I want to own more shops than anybody else.'

It was strange. In his business dealings he was said to be sharp and decisive but, when you met him, he seemed paralysed with shyness. He had a most beautiful face, in the James Dean manner, with curly hair and hollowed cheeks, and solitary eyes, and he spoke in a curious, high-pitched key. When he shook your hand, he couldn't look at you.

Yet his ambitions were infinite. When he had worked in Notting Hill Gate, he had doubled as a night-waiter in Fortes, saving up to start on his own and, once he'd achieved that much, he used to put in a hundred hours a week. 'That's why he was a genius, because he followed his obsessions,' says Michael Fish, who once worked for him. 'He was like Picasso or Michelangelo or Adolf Hitler.'

Today, looking back, he can give no explanation of what drove him, or why he cared so passionately. 'It was something I believed in,' he says and that, more or less, is as verbal as he gets.

My own guess, however, is that his hunger was for success in general, rather than for recognition as a designer or for anything specifically to do with clothes. As I see him, he had a built-in restlessness and couldn't ever have settled for orthodoxy – a steady job and a semi-detached. Somehow or other, he had to find an escape route and menswear provided it. No doubt he also liked clothes, enjoyed selling and designing them but, if circumstances had been different, he might equally well have been a Pop manager, or an adman, or a property developer. Still, having made his choice, he immersed himself totally.

Because he was young himself, he perceived that basic changes could only come through teenagers. Adults were too scared ever to take a lead; kids had no such inhibitions and Stephen set out to get them.

He was not successful immediately. Holed up in Beak Street he struggled for a time and then, just as he was getting himself established, he went to lunch and left the electric fire on. By the time he got back, his entire stock was in flames.

He wasn't sidetracked for long. Within a few months, he had moved round the corner into Carnaby Street and reopened. This time he was in direct competition with Vince and he won. Everything that he did, he did it faster and cheaper. At first, his trade was largely camp but soon pop stars like Cliff Richard and Billy Fury came to him, bringing their fans behind them.

To reach the teenage market, Stephen turned His Clothes into something equivalent to rock 'n' roll. All the traditional standards – wear, finish, craftsmanship – were made secondary to the instant, and he changed styles monthly, weekly, even daily.

He also cut his prices. On average, he charged £7 to £10 for jackets, £3 to £5 for trousers and about the same for shirts, and compared to John Michael or Vince, this worked out at around half as cheap again.

Above all, he made his shops like amusement arcades. He had records blaring as loud as they would go, kaleidoscopic window displays, garments hung around the open doorways and spilling out across the pavements, in imitation of St Tropez. For the first time shopping ceased to be a chore. Instead of ducking in and out quickly, kids would go along especially, as a treat, and trail slowly along the parade, fingering the clothes in the doorways, dazzled by colours and deafened by Pop. Inside, there was more, infinite brightness and newness and glamour, and they would be drawn in helplessly. Clothes had become an adventure.

There were other ploys, lots of gimmicks and publicity stunts. But this was all embellishment. Underneath, the central equation was that, every time you walked past a John Stephen window, there was something new and loud in it, and when you counted out your money, you found you could afford it.

Very quickly he had opened a second branch, also in Carnaby Street and, seeing the signals, other boutiques like Donis and Domino Male moved in alongside him. By the end of 1961, Stephen had four shops, and had expanded on to Regent Street, and Carnaby Street had turned into a definite menswear colony.

Somewhere along the line, the word boutique had come in, although no one now seems sure who used it first. Partly, it was used because a lot of early Carnaby Street styles were French-inspired; partly out of camp; but in any case, it caught on immensely and, by the early sixties, even the multiple stores were calling departments boutiques.

In 1962, a range of His Clothes was modelled by Billy Walker, the heavyweight, and this was also important. Walker, at the time, was still in his Golden Boy phase, the great hope of British boxing, and he was worshipped so much that not even pink denims could sully his manhood. Huge blow-ups of him in drag appeared in all Stephen's windows, and in the press, and they worked wonders. From then on, Carnaby Street seemed almost respectable.

But the floodgates didn't open fully until after the Beatles. In 1962, they cut 'Love Me Do'. By the following summer, Beatlemania was raging at full force and the great teenage boom was under way, a cult that turned Carnaby Street from a backwater into a massive worldwide madness.

6 DAYS IN THE LIFE – JONATHON GREEN

Green has produced two fine books on the '60s but this, his oral history of the decade, is far stronger on Modernism. That's because he's gone to the source, the ones with the real know how.

DAVID MAY: What sent you to London from the provinces was the whole mod culture, which swept aside the early-60s beatniks. Mods were always intellectual. There was always a large gay element in it. On Saturday afternoon we'd go to get our hair done in the women's hair-dressers. Then we'd go out in the evening, dancing. Saturday afternoon we'd go down the town, buying some new piece of clothing. We didn't fight rockers, we were far more interested in some guy's incredible shoes, or his leather coat. But underneath this, one did read Camus. *The Outsider*, there it was, it explained an awful lot. A sort of Jean Genet criminal lowlife was also important. These were the outlaw figures. People who went out and stole and so on. And until the drug squad appeared in 1967 there was this period, for me from the age of fourteen to eighteen, when the police didn't impinge at all. We lived in this whole other world; getting stoned and hoping to get laid. And soul music. And what had to happen, for everyone, was that you had to move away.

STEVE SPARKS: I was a mod. I was one of the original mods, one of the real Wardour Street mods. Not the post-commercialised mods, but back then when it was all existentialism and rhythm and blues. There were like 120 mods, period. Everyone else were the commercialised Carnaby Street mods. They came from Ilford, East London and North London; The Noreik Club axis, a Tottenham club; and a coffee bar in Ilford called the Mocha. Those were the centres around which mod grew. The Who, of course, were Shepherd's Bush, but that came later. I ran a folk club and I used to run a club in the back room of this pub in Barking and we used to have the High Numbers, as they were then, and all those Rik Gunnell Flamingo people … Georgie Fame, Geno Washington and the Ram-Jam band, that whole R&B/ Flamingo sort of music. Pete Townshend used to punch holes in the ceiling of the club with his guitar. Amphetamines, Jean-Paul Sartre and John Lee Hooker. That was being a mod. And the clothes. Church's brogues … I still wear Church's brogues, the only thing left from those days. Silk and Mohair suits.

7 MARC BOLAN – MARK PAYTRESS

Great detail concerning one of London's earliest Mods from Bolan's main biographer. Check also the Frankie Laine quote. 'Knock my talent if you must but not my tailor.' Pure Mod thinking.

In a memorable interview with *Rolling Stone* magazine, conducted at the peak of his career, Mark told a story which freeze-framed British subculture in transition. Sitting on his doorstep dressed in his black drainpipes, his chukka boots and his Everly Brothers-style blue-striped shirt with its collar characteristically turned up, Mark Feld gazed adoringly as one of those heavy Stoke Newington Teds passed by, radiating perfection from the crease in his duck's arse hairstyle down to the toes of his winklepicker boots. His envy was scarcely containable. Then the figure of one Martin Kauffman strolled past, dressed in baggy ginger Harris-tweed trousers and a pair of green handmade pointed shoes with side-buckles. He also wore a short dark green blazer and his hair-style had a radical centre parting, with the fringe flopping into his eyes.

Within weeks, Mark had thrown himself headlong into this sartorial battlefield where style was no longer merely an adjunct to the music you listened to. Martin Kauffman may only have been on his way to work when he happened to pass the Felds' home, but to his impassioned observer, the flair he'd shown in perfecting such a meticulously crafted self-image endowed him with a sense of individuality that not even the drudgery of labour could dampen. Kauffman was undoubtedly an early Modernist –

one of a group of obsessive stylists who developed out of the modern jazz clubs – and the idea that emancipation came through close attention to the details of dress was the essence of what later came to be called mod culture.

The fading of the Teds and the gradual emergence of the Modernists represented far more than merely a change of tailor. While both subcultures flourished in roughly the same working-class areas, and both screamed out to be recognised, the Teds' uniform was exactly that – a uniform. It consisted of little more than buying the correct outfit and adorning it with the appropriate accessories. The Modernists, meanwhile, were nothing if not eclectic. Instead of sticking to one readily recognisable style, they sought continually to adapt and evolve their dress, combining functional garments designed for the country gentleman with sportswear, ladies' fashions with suits aimed at the city gent. What lay behind this obsessive one-upmanship was the new spirit of competitive individualism that had supplanted the austerity years and, in this respect, Modernist culture in its pure form marked a sharp break with the insular, herd-like outlook of the Teds' world. It should not be confused with what generally became known as the mid-sixties mod 'movement', by which time the ideology – not to mention the styles – had altered considerably.

The self-obsessed almost exclusively male world to which Martin Kauffman and his ilk adhered offered infinite possibilities to Mark Feld. It gave him free rein to turn his role-playing in on himself, allowing him to indulge his manifest narcissism, while also satisfying the compulsion to keep redesigning himself in ever more spectacular guises. It was shameless consumerism – but creative with it. To the young stylists, puritan restraint had gone out with band-leader Victor Sylvester and 'austerity' Chancellor Stafford Cripps.

Frances Perrone noticed the change in her tenants' son. 'He used to leave the house dressed up to the nines,' she recalls, 'He'd become a real little flash boy, that Mark, and he never went anywhere without his rolled-up umbrella. He'd still have his radiogram blaring out, but his room would be dominated by this great big clothes line that stretched from one wall to the other. I used to have a shoe shop in Stoke Newington Church Street and he was forever asking me to make him shoes. I'd got him some made in lizard-skin or snake-skin, but then he got a bit too much. He wanted shoes every other day.'

Mark was too young to have been taken seriously at first by the elder Modernists, as they vied with each other for attention. When he was eleven, in 1958, the 'Italian look' – square-shouldered 'bumfreezer' jackets with narrow lapels and two or three covered buttons; narrow trousers without turn-ups – had already signalled a new peak in teenage sophistication and modernity. Frankie Laine had brought the style to Britain back in 1955, and was roundly savaged by the critics for wearing it at the London Palladium, that near-sacred epicentre of British popular culture. So much for variety. Nevertheless, the pre-pubescent Mark Feld, still without the figure to wear a suit convincingly, pestered his mother for an Italian-style outfit. She took him to a local tailor, but her son's specific instructions regarding the cut left the outfitter flabbergasted.

Frankie Laine had told his adversaries, 'Knock my talent if you must, but not my tailor.' Mark Feld knew he couldn't rely on the goodwill of neighbours or the incompetence of local tradesmen if he really wanted to make it in style. Whereas he'd previously only been familiar with his own Stoke Newington/ Stamford Hill/Clapton/Hackney area and the immediate vicinity of his mother's stall in Soho, having to seek out cheap, efficient tailors widened Mark's territory. A train or bus trip would take him all the way to Alfred Bilgorri of Bishopsgate, near Liverpool Street Station, though if he travelled by bus, he could break the journey to check out Connick's boys' shop in Kingsland Road, Dalston, one of the few places that sold Levi's in his small size. Another regular haunt was a tailor in Leman Street in the heart of the Feld family's old stamping ground in Whitechapel, while further afield was Borowick's of Bow, at the intersection of Mile End Road and Grove Road. For footwear, Mark occasionally used a Greek shoemaker in Robert Street, Euston, until he discovered Stan Bartholomew's in Battersea, and later, the children's department of Ravel in Wardour Street. There were also trips to Anello & Davide, the famous Covent Garden ballet shoe shop, where Mark and his new West End friend, Jeff Dexter (who he first encountered at the Lyceum Ballroom in 1960), bought après-ski boots. A few years later, these reasonably priced and simply made items of footwear with the elasticated sides took off as 'Beatle Boots'.

Mark often summed up his youth by bragging that he had always been a star, 'even if it was only being the star of three streets in Hackney'. To the few close friends in Stoke Newington who shared his hopes, he probably was. Harry remembers his younger brother never being able to pass a mirror, but such extreme vanity was ultimately worthless unless he was able to exhibit what he'd created. Stamford Hill, with the Fairsports amusement arcade (known by the locals as the 'schtip' house; literally, 'to take your money'), cinema, bowling alley and the salt beef bar, became his regular catwalk. Here, he'd meet up with other local shmatte fiends, including Eric Hall, Midiey 'Modern' Turner, Gerry Goldstein and two older boys, Peter Sugar and Michael Simmonds.

The ultra-modern world inhabited by Mark and his friends contrasted sharply with Stamford Hill's formidable population of Hassidic Jews. Highly visible in their beaver hats, alpaca cloaks, untrimmed beards and long side ringlets, the religious orthodoxy of this tight-knit community manifested itself in a desperate attempt to cling to the eighteenth century lifestyle of their East European ancestors.

Another vital part of the local 'scene' was the network of youth clubs which, more often than not, were affiliated to the many synagogues in the area. Helen Shapiro remembers Mark making an appearance at her local meeting-place in Clapton. 'He came in with his crowd from Stamford Hill Jewish youth club, who were rivals of ours, and I hadn't seen him for a while. The change was unbelievable. He was very slim, obviously taller, and was dressed from head to toe in his Modernist clothes: bumfreezer jacket, button-down shirt, all the gear. He was obviously the leader of this gang and he came in and took the place over. We all thought, "Who does he think he is?", he was so sure of himself. But he always had a strong personality, even when he was nine.' Her cousin Susan Singer also remembers the transformation. 'Most of us were afraid to go too far,' she says, 'but not Mark. I must say he wasn't aggressive with it. In fact he was always very friendly and everyone at the dances liked him. I thought he was lovely.'

Jeff Dexter records a different response. 'He was hated – precisely because he looked so good. Everyone hated anyone who they felt had one up on them. People always tried to pick a fight with you if they felt you were competition. And we were surrounded by a lot of very rough firms then. A lot of the mods would dress up in their posh clothes and then go out and punch shit out of each other. Mark often pretended he was out for a fight.'

Jeff Dexter, like Mark, was absorbed in a scene that revolved around teenagers who were often much older and much bigger than him. It wasn't easy if you were young and small for your age to command respect in places like the Lyceum, where you had to pass six foot four inch bouncers before you could even enter. 'You had to be sixteen to get in,' Dexter recalls. 'We were only thirteen or fourteen, and probably looked no older than eleven, but we both had as much front as Woolworths. Mark always came across as a very smart chap with a great sense of dress. He stood out because he was little and he looked immaculate. But when you were small, you had to pretend that you were tougher than you were to stave off the aggravation, because you'd often get picked on. Mark always acted like he could fight a giant.

'I remember one incident at the Lyceum where he got into a bit of aggravation and he did get beaten. The other guy got thrown out, but Mark ran off, climbed out of the loo window, smartened himself up, and then strolled back in as if he'd beaten the guy to a pulp. But he hadn't. It wasn't until about a year later that he told me the truth.'

Small stature was also a problem for Mark and Jeff when it came to finding the right clothes in their size, which made tailors like Bilgorri doubly essential. But a trip to Bilgorri, whose reputation was such that many well-known East End gangsters refused to shop anywhere else, didn't come cheaply. 'I know that Mark always had fashion at his fingertips. Whether they were light fingers, I don't know,' says Harry Feld. Mark always recalled this era with fondness, and there is little reason to doubt his own explanation as to how he funded his shopping sprees. 'I was quite a villain,' he told Spencer Leigh in 1976, 'although I never hurt anybody. It came about because I was really into clothes, I mean, obsessively into clothes. I was about twelve and I'd steal or hustle motorbikes to pay for them. Clothes were all that mattered to me.'

He probably traded hijacked scooters which, by the early sixties, were a fashionable commodity among teenagers. They also provided useful getaway vehicles, for impoverished stylists. Mark once recalled a mass raid on a store in Whitechapel where, he claimed, forty Levi's-obsessed youngsters 'liberated' an entire stock of the much-coveted American jeans. His fellow looters scooted off without him and he was left, heart pounding, running for the nearest bus with the booty under his jumper. They'd invariably be a pair of 505s, which were identical to 501s but featured a zip instead of a button fly. Fumbling with buttons was slow, ungainly, and let in an unwelcome draught when you were out on a scooter run.

The other solution to Mark's cash problem was to buy items off the shelf cheaply, then get them customised at home. It was a trick he'd learnt from his mother, who had often transformed an old skirt into pairs of trousers for the boys. Jeff Dexter (who by this time had been plucked from obscurity and was dancing professionally with the Cyril Stapleton Band) often shopped with Mark at stores as unfashionable as C&A and Woolworths, where they'd invariably find something in the children's department which could then be taken home and tailored to suit.

It was thrift, coupled with the insatiable urge to defy uniformity, which prompted the Modernist scene to take off in new directions, and the relative popularity of the 'Italian look' soon gave way to all manner of sartorial combinations. All Modernists aspired to look sharp, in what was a symbolic refusal of their class position. The cult of the cloth also reflected the drive towards upward mobility, which befitted a nation that had been nudging close to full employment for several years. For young obsessives like Mark and Jeff, looking sharp wasn't the half of it: to their kind, staying sharp was the only goal worth achieving. If that meant personally supervising often minuscule alterations to a garment, or changing outfits twice, four, five times a day, then that was what had to be done.

When all-day Sunday sessions at the Lyceum became overcrowded, Mark (who was never much of a regular anyway) would turn disdainfully towards Jeff and say, 'Too many mods here.' There has always been an uncomfortable contradiction between the avowed personal expression of subcultural style, and the fact of belonging to a subculture, and nowhere is this anomaly better expressed than with the Individualists of 1961-2. The term never really entered into mainstream language, but it was bandied about by the Modernist vanguard in a bid to avoid becoming part of any coherent style. An Individualist – which in effect Mark was – would take the straight mod gear as a starting point, convert it, then throw in something completely at odds with the rest of the outfit. Mark's Stamford Hill gang, some of whom were becoming known as 'Faces' – the ultimate accolade among the Mod fraternity – picked up on this drive towards total originality, and before long, those outside the close-knit network of 'firms' had begun to take notice too.

In September 1962, three of these Faces made it into the pages of *Town*, then *the* lifestyle magazine for men (its only competitor being *Playboy*). Before Michael Heseltine and Clive Labovitch acquired it for Cornmarket Press in 1960, the publication was known as *Man About Town*, and it was only after a radical redesign by Tom Wolsey, and the decision to streamline its title (thus managing to convey a few all-important associated meanings – chic, youth, modernity), that *Town* really began to revel in the deification of affluence. A new breed of photographers, Terry Donovan, Terry Duffy, David Bailey, even future underground guru John 'Hoppy' Hopkins, had their early work featured in its pages; artists like David Hockney were sympathetically profiled; and only very occasionally would an old killjoy like Malcolm Muggeridge be invited to pen an article that threatened to spoil the party.

The theme of the September 1962 issue was 'The Young Take The Wheel'. What are they like? What do they do? What do they want? *Town* enquired, and reporter Peter Barnsley and photographer Donald McCullin (himself a veteran of the Teds scene) were despatched to Stamford Hill to find out. There they found two twenty-year-olds, Michael Simmonds and Peter Sugar, and fourteen-year-old Mark Feld. *Town* called them 'Faces Without Shadows', presumably because the pace of a Face's lifestyle was too intense to cast one. Certainly that was the impression the article sought to create, and the trio were quoted at length to back it up.

In spite of the professed desire to live in a perpetual present, Mark, who was described as 'the most remarkable of the three', showed an early compulsion towards self-mythology. 'Remember three years ago?' he asked his mates. 'It was easy then. We used to go round on scooters in Levi's and leather jackets. It was a lot easier then.' The vision of a twelve-year-old boy dressed to kill on the back of a bike in the streets of Hackney obviously impressed Barnsley. So did Feld's snappy replies to his questioning. He made Mark the star of the article, and McCullin displayed him prominently in six of the ten accompanying photographs.

The well-scrubbed Face from Stoke Newington Common used his moment well, combining arrogance, fantasy and a meticulous knowledge of the scene in equal measure. *Town* reported:

> 'You got to be different from the other kids,' says Feld. 'I mean, you got to be two steps ahead. The stuff that half the haddocks you see around are wearing I was wearing years ago. A kid in my class came up to me in his new suit, an Italian box it was. He says, "Just look at

the length of your jacket," he says. "You're not with it," he says. "I was wearing that style two years ago," I said. Of course they don't like that.'

According to the rules of the day, Mark's conceit was probably justified in that excerpt, but sometimes his embellishments to a story bore no resemblance to reality at all. Take the following passage from *Town*, where a debate on the lack of good London tailors arouses Mark's imagination:

> 'They aren't good on shoulders either,' says Feld. 'They can't make good shoulders like those French shoulders. I brought a jacket back from Paris – I was in Paris with my parents but I didn't like it much – and this jacket was just rubbish over there but it's great here. Great shoulders.'

Harry emphatically states that the family never went to Paris.

The piece offers a fascinating insight into the minds of the young pleasure seekers, and scratched below the surface just enough to reveal the motor that fuelled the 'exhausting race', the race that the writer was so certain would end in defeat. Had Richard Hoggart, and other radical critics of mass culture read the article, they would have been horrified. Gone were the old values of the working class, where the spirit of community, generosity and modesty prevailed. In their place had stepped rampant individualism, a mean-spirited competitiveness and excessive vanity.

The new gods were the likes of John Stephen, a young salesman at Vince's in Newburgh Street, who'd established his own clothes shop round the corner in Carnaby Street by the turn of the decade and had been doing a roaring trade with the likes of the Stamford Hill Faces. 'All those shops and still only twenty-six or something,' sighed Stark. No matter how or why: success was what mattered. Even Cliff Richard and Adam Faith were still on his mind. 'I suppose they're had-its in a way but they've done something. They've made their way at something,' he said.

When it came to issues that extended beyond the much-derided 'baggy seats' and the virtues of women's hatpins, the three young peacocks showed a remarkable nonchalance. Michael Simmonds opined that the 'Ban the Bomb lot' were dead right, but he'd never march with them. Mark supported them too. 'It's all exhibitionist, isn't it? I'm all for that,' he said.

Politics mattered little to mods, but the trio from N16 knew which side they were on:

> 'I'm a Conservative,' said Peter Sugar. 'I mean Conservatives are for the rich, aren't they, and everybody wants to be rich, really, don't they?'
>
> 'They've been in a long time and they done all right,' said Simmonds.
>
> 'Yeah, like he says, they're for the rich, really, so I'm for them,' says Feld.
>
> 'Of course I don't know much about it,' says Sugar.

The equation was simple. The Conservative Party looked after the rich and the sophisticated. No matter that Mark was sharing a cold bedroom with plaster coming off the walls and his wet clothes dripping water on to the lino: economic realities faded into the background as the truth of his own importance grew ever more apparent. It was politics by association, and Faces nailed their made-to-measure banner to the glamorous and wealthy. As Jeff Dexter says, 'Even though you were an oik at heart, you wanted to be classy. It was the original wannabe culture. Wannabe boys, wanna create, wannabe rich, wannabe famous, wannabe loved, wannabe known.'

As the fashions of the Individualists/Faces/Stylists developed, this sense of aspiring towards the rich was more closely reflected in the dress, and coexisted with the overriding need to create a look of perfection. The immediate antecedent for this process was the movement of a few of the original rock 'n' rollers into the jazz clubs, who sought to replace rebellion with sophistication. They quickly picked up on the rather ill-fitting, slightly cramped Ivy League clothes worn by many of the visiting American jazz musicians. Unbeknown to the clubgoers, Ivy League dress was originally based on traditional English lines, being little more than an Americanised version of what an English undergraduate would wear, with minor modifications such as the introduction of button-down collars. America's yearning for the trappings of British culture was then exported back to Britain, where it fused with the Italian and French looks and formed the backbone of the Modernist style.

It was probably the features editor, a young Michael Parkinson, who decided to play safe when captioning the photographs in *Town*, which were given a decidedly – and appropriate – grainy cast. The three youths were portrayed in a variety of outfits, the details of which were obviously too acute even for the staff of the country's top men's magazine. But the mix of idiosyncrasy and tradition was self-evident. One memorable still, depicting the dark-suited Simmonds and Sugar leaning against a Soho wall, with a defiant jawed Mark Feld in the foreground, caught this fusion well. Mark is dressed in an immaculate hacking jacket, complete with slanting pockets – a garment usually associated with the horse-riding Hoorays from the shires. However, it has been modified and his customised jacket is unique by virtue of its elongated lapel. The formal trousers, boasting razor-sharp creases, and his collar and tie are less spectacular, but this particular Face's crowning glory is his leather waistcoat. Leather goods were virtually impossible to find in Mark's size (and extremely expensive), but he had managed to persuade Mrs Perrone in the flat downstairs to make him something to his specific requirements. It was a highly prized item, and proved versatile enough to be worn with his best clothes for a stroll around Soho, or as part of a casual combination for roughing it down by the Grand Union Canal.

Years later, Mark described this first taste of public recognition as 'a bummer article'. The reason? '[It] came out about seven months after they'd actually come down to see me and taken the pictures.' During that time, a Face's wardrobe would have been completely transformed – several times over.

Jeff Dexter always thought Mark's crowning glory was his thick, buoyant head of hair, which he wore in a particularly severe style around the time of the *Town* pictures. 'There was an awful lot of what used to be called horizon line around at that time,' he recalls, 'which was a parted college boy haircut raised at the top of the head. Mark's hair naturally raised in the middle so he always looked absolutely immaculate during that period. I envied that little lift in the middle a lot and spent many hours with a hair-dryer in front of a mirror trying to get mine to do the same. After all that effort, it inevitably fell down flat on my forehead after I'd been dancing.' Mark never had that trouble. Besides, he rarely danced.

8 DAYS IN THE LIFE – JONATHON GREEN

DAVID GOODMAN: At school me and my friend Phil de Newman were the mods. His brother Colin was the real head mod, the stylist, and when he was still at the school we were just third class tickets. It was basically very difficult to be a mod at boarding school. All the pair of us wanted to do was get out there and get a scooter and get some money to get some really nice snappy duds and stuff. We used to spend hours drawing shirts with button-down collars and design them in different shapes and draw paisley patterns and they wouldn't let me take art because I drew mods on scooters instead of drawing landscapes. 'Draw a landscape,' and I'd draw a seaside resort with mods with parkas on.

They brought in half-term holidays and we would head straight for Soho. Before we went we'd spend hours mapping out where we wanted to go – the Palladium, Drury Lane, Anello and Davide where I'd buy my Beatle boots, the 2i's coffee bar. It wasn't a rock and roll haunt any more but it was the first time I'd ever heard Prince Buster singing 'Madness' and another classic ska record called 'Carolina' by the Folk Brothers.

JOHN MARSH: What appealed to me about the mods was the physical, material style. I was totally sold on the look. Among certain mods a real dedication to pleasure existed. The kinds of pleasures were fairly basic, and rather alien to the hippie idea of pleasure, but above all there was the music. R&B, Motown, some of the jazz. There were some mods who liked it only because it was fashionable, but there was a hardcore of old mod

49

types who were dedicated to it.

I was also in sympathy with the ideas of the beats, but loathed their physical appearance. Whereas it was vice versa with the mods, whose grubbier, more down-market excesses I loathed. Any attempt by me to get the two to co-exist, even in my own mind, was doomed to failure because the two were basically antipathetic. The mod thing was the first time in which I realised that there was somehow something wrong somewhere.

I never could come to terms with hippies and I never really was a hippie or part of that counterculture other than in the most peripheral sense. As a mod, what was happening, and where it was happening, and where it was going and all the rest of it was all kind of understandable. You were part of a certain sort of culture and group because of the possession of so many suits, how much chrome there was on your scooter, how many girls you'd had knee-tremblers with against the back wall of various West End clubs. It was understandable: where you stood, who you were, what you were was all fairly clearly defined.

STEVE SPARKS: Mod has been much misunderstood. Mod is always seen as this working-class, scooter-riding precursor of skinheads, and that's a false point of view. Mod before it was commercialised was essentially an extension of the beatniks. It comes from 'modernist', it was to do with modern jazz and to do with Sartre. It was to do with existentialism, the working-class reaction to existentialism. Marc Feld (who became Marc Bolan) was an early example of what was the downfall of mod, which was the attraction of people who didn't understand what it was about to the clothes. Marc Feld was only interested in the clothes, he was not involved in thinking. Mind you, it's quite hard to think on twenty Smith Kline and French Drinamyl.

MALDWYN THOMAS: I came across Marc several times, in his Marc Feld era, as one of the faces at the Scene. I kept bumping into him. I was going down the tailors and getting mohair suits. All sorts of wild suits: three-piece suits that weren't three-piece: the trousers and the vest were all in one, like a catsuit. Zoot suits, pork-pie hats. This was serious business – very serious being a face, Those sort of drugs, amphetamines, make things very serious anyway. I started going to the Scene when I was about fourteen. Off Wardour Street, it was a mod club. You spent all night at the Scene, you took blues, you went home in the morning.

PEARCE MARCHBANK: There were pills at the Scene. There used to be straight Coke and expensive Coke. Expensive Coke had something in it, probably amphetamine. I was there during a police raid once. Suddenly when you walked across the room there were pills all over the floor.

9 "LONDON'S SPEEDING"

Shapiro's book on drugs and music, entitled Waiting For The Man *is essential gear and not just because it shares the same publisher as this book. I've never read such detail on Mods and speed.*

The Beatles discovered what the rock 'n' rollers already knew and the rock musicians of the future would soon find out, that amphetamines were 'working drugs'. Nobody can play blind drunk and those who tried playing on acid often found themselves deep in conversation with microphone stands and speaker cabinets. Speed (and later cocaine) works by giving musicians the courage to get out there and sufficient edge to keep going throughout the performance. But trying to talk to the audience can be a mistake, when Elvis was taking large amounts of speed to trim down for a tour audiences were subjected to long rambling monologues between songs.

This is amphetamine use in a purely functional role. For the mods, amphetamines were symbolically enshrined at the heart of their subculture, fitting into a discrete universe, a system of magical correspondences in which all objects – clothes, music, scooters and drugs – had a precise relationship with one another. Each item was taken from the straight world and redefined within a homogenous cosmos; amphetamines were the subcultural adhesive which joined lifestyles and values: the functional springboard for the frantic activity of staying up, buying clothes, riding and fixing scooters, and dancing.

'Mod' was a catch-all phrase which encompassed a variety of

styles, contributing to a media-created image of 'Swinging London.' It should have been called 'Speeding London'; the amphetamine-induced arrogance, edginess, narcissism and freneticism of mod culture was reflected right through the art, music and fashion of the period. London's Pop Art scene was like a giant Roy Lichstenstein painting – POW!! ZAP!! But as with all amphetamine 'runs' there came the inevitable crash. Like the merry-go-round at the end of Hitchcock's *Strangers on a Train* the scene collapsed and London was probably a duller place for it.

But when it all started, the mods were the upfront ambassadors. By the time the style had been castrated by the High Street entrepreneurs for furious but safe consumption, the mods had 'turned neatness into an art form'. They came from a post-war British working-class attitude to smartness, best described as 'flash'. The spivs (George Cole as 'Flash Harry' in St Trinian's films, Arthur Daley as a young man) were followed by Teds who hijacked a failed attempt by Saville Row to revive Edwardian elegance for the aristocracy, adding string ties and slick hairdos to a taste for American rock 'n' roll and the Mississippi steamboat gambler.

Mods, too, took some inspiration from the States in taste and their attempt to re-create the sartorial coolness of the black hipster. However, they looked to the Continent, particularly Italy, for the clothes themselves.

Amphetamines promote a sense of controlled anger (which is why they have proved so popular among American footballers). The mod stance was undeniably uptight. They looked normal, but they weren't. They made wearing a suit and tie seem aggressive and threatening. Somehow too smart and too neat, they caused consternation among 'the straights', who saw their own conservative dress sense mocked. The worst thing that could happen to a mod was to have his parents understand him.

In 1961, 2½% of all NHS prescriptions were for amphetamines. Even so, mods made speed their own: it was youthful recreational use of amphetamines, not over-prescribing by GPs, that caused them to be controlled in drugs legislation passed in 1964 especially created for the purpose. Getting blocked on pills at weekends was what separated 'them from us'.

The relentless pursuit of fashion eclipsed everything else; food, drink and women didn't matter because speed killed the appetite for all three, which may account for the fact that the mod cult was predominantly male. Many mods had office jobs, paying around

£11 a week, most of which went on clothes and pills. Mod fashion was a microcosm of an industrial society which paid homage to the sacred cow of built-in obsolescence. A mod would spend three weeks' wages having vents put in or taken out of jackets, lapels widened or narrowed, knowing that three weeks later something else would be 'in', and mods would rather stay home than be seen out in last week's fashion. Probably no teenage style has paid such meticulous attention to the minutiae of its uniform, an obsession which had its counterpart in the way amphetamine users can get totally absorbed in mindless and trivial occupations like washing a plate.

For mods, speed also had purely functional applications. First was fighting. The early mods had no time for violence but the hysterical press reporting of the first major mod-rocker clash at Clacton on Easter Monday 1964 became a self-fulfilling prophecy. This was the first time most people had heard about mods or rockers and the press instantly created a new breed of 'folk devils' to rival Teds and razor gangs. The press reports were littered with words and phrases like 'battle', 'attack', 'siege', 'screaming mob' and 'orgy of destruction'. The press exaggerated and distorted every aspect of the confrontation, conveying the impression that the fracas was strictly polarized on mod and rocker lines. In fact initially the clashes were more between rival gangs from London and the Home Counties. Only later, in some of the more bloody disturbances when it had become fashionable to be either mod or rocker, did these battles take on the lines of a clash of subcultures. At that point, the mod underground, a cool, understated bunch of natty dressers, became media darlings. Nothing really subversive ever got the *Sunday Times* Colour Supplement treatment. In the hunt for the ideal mod to interview, the *Sunday Times* came up with 'Denzil', who said 'Pills make you edgy and argumentable'; it made them hyper-sensitive to the possibilities of action and generated the desire to go looking for trouble. Having got totally wired up on pills, mods had to find trouble to release the frustration of what felt like an arrested orgasm. And after the way the press handled the Easter/Whitsun '64 incidents, it was obvious that any right-thinking mods or rockers out for some free publicity to shock the nation would get together at appointed times and places 'predicted' by the press, in the sure knowledge that the cameras would be ready and waiting.

Denzil had more to say – an average week in the life of the ideal London mod:

Monday night	Dancing at the Mecca, the Hammersmith Palais, the Purley Orchard or the Streatham Locarno
Tuesday	Soho and the Scene Club
Wednesday	Marquee night
Thursday	Washing hair (which had to be dried using a dryer with a hood)
Friday	Back at the Scene
Saturday afternoon	Clothes and record-buying
Saturday night	The All Nighter at the Flamingo

It is unlikely that any mod ever kept up a regime like that for long however much speed he took. It all cost money and although mods were the most affluent teenagers to date, the money had to run out some time. Nevertheless the diary does demonstrate the importance of music and the club scene to all mods, whether 'hard core' or 'weekenders'.

In Britain, the club scene has always provided the main platform for the development of the new genres of musical taste from traditional jazz to punk rock. The only significant competition has been from the college circuit in the affluent late sixties, where many of the underground or 'progressive' bands like Jethro Tull built up their early following. The clubs and pubs also suffered in the early seventies from a vacuum which was left after most British rock bands went to play large arenas in America. Pub bands like Dr Feelgood and Kilburn and the High Roads helped promote a small-venue revival which finally took off with the arrival of punks. With the Beatles, northern clubs like the Cavern in Liverpool and the Twisted Wheel in Manchester, had already carved out for themselves a significant place in rock history, but much of the media and business interest during the sixties focused on London and the Soho club scene. That's where the music was to be found. And the drugs. Dark, subterranean dives, packed with people frantically dancing to loud music were an ideal setting for drug-dealing.

One of the main centres for speed-dealing was the Scene Club, situated in Ham Yard at 41 Great Windmill Street. The club was run by Ronan O'Rahilly, one-time manager of Alexis Korner's Blues Incorporated and a pioneer of pirate radio with Radio Caroline. Although O'Rahilly ran the Scene, it was part of the Nash gang club operation in Soho and hence a dangerous place to be.

The club had an interesting history. Several venues had existed on the site, including the Cy Laurie Club and the Piccadilly Jazz Club, where music entrepreneur Giorgio Gomelsky first saw the Rolling Stones. Back in the forties and early fifties, it was none other than the Club Eleven, where the first London club bust had taken place in 1950. As the Scene it was the place to be seen, as far as Mods were concerned. The DJ was Guy Stevens, who had the best American record collection in Britain, chock full of rare soul, blues and r&b discs. He co-ran Sue Records with Chris Blackwell and later produced for Mott the Hoople and the Clash.

O'Rahilly had the walls padded and cushions strewn everywhere, so that those who speeded to exhaustion could crash out. Two cousins who manned the door for a time had a habit of relieving patrons of their pill stash as they entered, pretending to flush them down the toilet and then recycling them. The dealing went on in the club, safe from prying eyes; Drinamyl pills were sold at 1/3d. (c. 6p) each, but were normally bought in fives, tens, twenties, fifties and hundreds.

In March 1967, *Oz* magazine spoke to two twenty-one-year-old dealers called Paul and Cliff. They had a joint income of up to £400 a week and both owned '66 Ford Zephyrs. A third of the money was passed to a godfather figure they called 'Big Sid', and they employed two West Indian minders with whom they shared a twenty-guinea-a-week flat (£21) in Chelmsford:

> Starting their work at the Marquee club they sell to a market of thirteen-year-old mods; after a meal they move into the clubs around Greek Street; then to a stand just outside Tiffany's at about one in the morning. When necessary they work a pitch in the Lyon's Cafés around Trafalgar Square; if on Sunday morning they have any pills remaining, they move into Chelsea where apparently tired debs are always a ready market. In conversation with one reporter as to the origin of the amphetamines, they said that some of their pills were knocked off, but most came as a regular supply through London docks – they weren't sure where, but 'Big Sid looks after that end.' In one weekend they never sell less than 3,000 pills and sometimes in excess of 6,000, undercutting other pushers by selling at 1/- each.

Another key club for the speed dealers in the early sixties was La Discotheque in Wardour Street. It was originally called El Condor, and from 1957-61 operated as an exclusive night spot frequented by British royalty. The club was owned by Raymond Nash and Peter Rachman, whose name has since become synonymous with racketeering landlords. Rachman sold the club to Tommy Yeardye and one of Rachman's own proteges, Peter Davies. However, the new club went bankrupt and reopened as the far more downmarket Discotheque. Hordes of young people replaced the upper middle class and the smattering of aristocrats. Rachman and Nash resumed control as joint shareholders. They installed a powerful lighting and sound system. Drinks were 5/- but the place was more awash with cheap amphetamines. A dealer dubbed 'Peter the Pill' forged another link between Rachman and the London amphetamine scene, as he was both a (if not the) major dealer in speed and one of Rachman's loyal soldiers.

The question of supply during this period is one that has never been fully investigated. Certainly most of the amphetamines in circulation around the clubs were manufactured drugs, not the product of illicit street laboratories. Nor, in view of the huge number of pills involved, could they simply have been spillage from over-prescribing by doctors. Individual youngsters may have obtained some from the medicine cupboard at home, but not dealers.

As these drugs invariably had the manufacturer's name SKF (Smith, Kline and French) stamped on them, those working with chronic amphetamine users in Soho came to the not unreasonable conclusion that vast quantities of drugs were finding their way directly to dealers via SKF employees pilfering from the factory and warehouses. At a meeting of the Society for the Study on Addiction in September 1966, one worker, Judith Piepe, got up and said so in public:

> Extensive security precautions in a factory cost a great deal of money. It is easy for anybody on the production line quietly to take a handful and augment their wages by selling them. The production cost of drugs like Drinamyl are very low and the cost in money to ensure better security arrangements is considered too high by the manufacturers. They do not consider the cost in suffering to young people.

Replying for SKF, a Mr Schrire said:

> In regard to the accusation that tablets are being stolen

from the manufacturing companies, I regard this as nonsense. The tablets are manufactured under stringent supervision and it is highly improbable that any quantities could be stolen from the factories in these circumstances.

At about this time, the press reported a Gloucestershire doctor as saying that amphetamines were being made by teenagers with O-level chemistry. He offered no evidence for this and the *Daily Mirror* rang various experts to check the story. One GP, Ian Pierce-James, stated that he was sure anyone with O-level chemistry could make amphetamine pills, but wondered how they managed to make the little moulds and stamp SKF on them!

Who were the dealers? To judge from Paul and Cliff's story, the operation was very lucrative and involved some crude dealer hierarchy. At the top may have sat members of Britain's most notorious criminal gangs of the sixties. They owned many of the West End clubs and would be unlikely to allow any profitable side action to be carried out in those clubs without taking some of the profits for themselves. In 1968, the Government introduced a system of NHS clinics supplying drugs to addicts in the hope of preventing organised crime setting up a widespread black market in illicit drugs. As we know, at best this system merely postponed the event, but it may have been that the gangs had already staked a claim in the illicit market prior to '68.

The clubs where speed was used and dealt ranged from the world famous to the here today, gone tomorrow. Despite its clean-cut image, the Marquee was a pill palace, catering for a younger mod set who were on the way home to bed, before the All Nighter session at the more sophisticated Flamingo Club got under way. The Flamingo provided mods with a chance to rub shoulders with black American airforce men on forty-eight-hour passes and dance to the black-inspired R&B of Georgie Fame and Zoot Money. Mods frequented the Last Chance, Le Kilt, La Poubelle and the Roaring Twenties, a basement place in Carnaby Street, before the street became fashionable. Originally a failed attempt to persuade Jewish teenagers from the more expensive parts of North London to part with their money on Saturday nights, the club reopened as the Roaring Twenties, a black club where bluebeat first appeared together with pimps, prostitutes and the general mêlée of Soho wide-boys selling stolen watches and dodgy Jags. Tiles was another important venue, providing the meeting place for a lunchtime mod culture which Tom Wolfe called the Noonday Underground.

The Reverend Ken Leech was a well-known figure around Soho in the sixties. He cared for young people in trouble at the Centrepoint night shelter at St Anne's Church, and was a keen observer of life in Soho at the time, trusted and respected by all the disparate and volatile elements that made up the fascinating community.

> As you walked up Wardour Street and turned into D'Arblay Street, there was a very small area which you could walk round in ten minutes where there was a very heavy concentration of amphetamine clubs within yards of each other. You had in 1961, Le Douce, a gay club, directly opposite you had a club which changed its name several times but was most famous as the Subway. Then you had the Coffee Pot, which never closed (and where according to Richard Neville's *Playpower*, I'm always to be found!) Underneath that was the Huntsman and then opposite, in a smelly cul-de-sac between Wardour Street and Berwick Street, was Wardour Mews with the Limbo Club, the Granada and the Take Five.

And what of the music itself? There was really no such thing as mod music, rather music that mods liked. Mod was originally short for modernists and in musical terms that meant modern jazz. They also picked up on black R&B, soul and Jamaican bluebeat and in the tiny clubs mentioned above, danced frantically to chart stuff from the jukebox. But if any music came to represent the anger, frustration, brashness and arrogance of the mods, it was that of the Who.

Right at the start the Kinks were in competition with the Who to be the mods' living identification, the people's band, but in the end they couldn't compete with the Who's autodestruction and Townshend's anthems for a teenage wasteland. Nor did they have a Pete Meaden or a Kit Lambert.

Between them, Meaden and Lambert fashioned the Who's mod image; by inclination none of them was a mod. Meaden, a Drinamyl disciple and a face among the faces down at the Scene, became the Who's publicist and began the image-building whereby mods came to identify with the band. His short-lived renaming of the Who to the High Numbers was meant to indicate the state Meaden and the Who were in most of the time. Kit Lambert, who seemed to be able to function only under the influence of uppers or downers, depending on what image he needed to project at the time, completed the process with trips to Carnaby Street and the hairdressers. Townshend later said, 'The mod image was forced on us. It was dishonest.' To keep their credibility intact, the band would watch what dance steps the mod audiences were doing and re-create them on stage, so that another audience would think the Who had invented them. The management of Kit Lambert and Chris Stamp was ideal, as Keith Moon explained: 'These people were perfect for us, because there's me, bouncing about, full of pills, full of everything I could get my hands on … and there's Pete, very serious, never laughing, always cool, a grasshead … Kit and Chris were the epitome of what we were.'

The audience responded to the Who on a number of levels. First there was the aggression. 'We were all pillheads,' said Daltrey. 'We were probably the most aggressive group that's ever happened in England.' But the truth was they were not all pillheads to the same extent, Daltrey least of all. The root cause of much of the frisson which sparked off fist fights in the band and generated such excitement on stage was precisely Daltrey's anger at Townshend's and Moon's drug intake, which often sent them out of control. But after Townshend had hit his guitar on the ceiling of the Railway Hotel in Wealdstone, Harrow and had to finish the job by wrecking it to save face, being 'out of control' became the Who's trademark – swirling arms, swirling mikes and a demolition derby driven by the immense volume. The fans responded to the physical presence of the Who; shrill, cutting guitar over a raw, open-nerved tension-ridden pounding and crashing. The Who always had more amplification than anyone else and along with Ginger Baker, Keith Moon pioneered the use in rock of huge double bass drumkits with a forest of tom-toms and cymbals. Then there were Townshend's songs; 'I Can't Explain', in retrospect not the Moon-and-June love song Townshend thought he'd written, but a statement on the inability to communicate much about thoughts and feelings; 'My Generation', with the stutter of an amphetamine freak which Daltrey didn't want to sing at first; 'Anyway, Anyhow, Anywhere' – 'Nothing gets in my way, not even locked doors'; 'Substitute', about all the insecurities beneath the desperate need to keep up appearances and stand behind the image.

The mods were regarded, and regarded themselves, as an army, a unified body which often acted as one, yet at the same time each mod saw himself as an island; speed gave each individual a razor-edged identity and a pin-sharp sense of his place in the world. And this was the achievement of the Who, the reason why, despite the manufactured image, they symbolized to mods what being a mod was all about, 'the ultimate instance of individuality acquiring its deepest meaning from interaction with others'. The Who 'balanced the tension between individual vision and collective achievement without ever bothering to conceal the stress it caused – and this became part and parcel of their image.'

Although the Kinks had initially vied with the Who as the mods' band, it was the Small Faces who carried the flame for mod subculture in its death throes, inevitably sucked into the mainstream of sanitized pop. The Small Faces were genuine mods and, just as the Yardbirds took over from the Stones, the Small Faces assumed cult status on the club circuit from the Who. They didn't stay there for long. Their first single, 'What 'Cha Gonna Do About It?' reached No. 14 in the charts in August 1965 and in January 1966 they had a major success with 'Sha La La La Lee'. But from the point of view of this story, 1967 was their most important year. In June 1967, with words like 'hippy', 'joint', 'acid' and 'psychedelic' dropping from everyone's lips, the Small Faces brought out 'Here Comes the Nice', an anthem to the pill-popping heyday of the mod. With the police and the media witch-hunting the Rolling Stones as satanic junkies, the Small Faces calmly strolled on to 'Top of the Pops' with 'Here comes the nice/He knows what I need/He's always there when I need some speed,' the rest of the song being one of the more blatant rhapsodies to the drug dealer as cult hero. Stevie Marriott said later, '"Here Comes the Nice" was a drug song, but no one sussed it, the whole point being if they don't suss it, it's cool ... we could do it on "Top of the Pops" and we did it to be rebellious in a way – to see what we could get away with.'

10   THE NOONDAY UNDERGROUND – TOM WOLFE

Tom Wolfe, the man behind New Journalism and one of America's greatest journalists, came to London and penned this amazing study of Modernism in full flower. It's from his book The Pump House Gang.

Just keep straight. Keep your desk straight, keep your Biros straight, keep your paper clips straight, keep your Scotch tape straight keep your nose straight keep your eyes straight keep your tie on straight keep your head on straight keep your wife on straight keep your life on straight and that is Leicester Square out there and that is a straight square and this is a straight office, making straight money – hey! –

– Noses straight up there!

– Line up those noses there! – there – is – an – office boy here, Larry Lynch, a 15-year-old boy from the Brixton section of London, staring up at the straight line of human noses. Occasionally someone – what the hell is it with this kid? Here he is, 15 years old, and he is dressed better than any man in the office. He has on a checked suit with a double-breasted waistcoat with a stepcollar on it and the jacket coming in at the waist about like so, and lapels like this and vents like this and flaps about so and trousers that come down close here and then flare out here, and a custom-made shirt that comes up like … *so* at the neckband, little things very few people would even know about, least of all these poor straight noses up here who make four times his pay and they never had a suit in their lives that wasn't off the peg. He is a working-class boy, and like most

working-class boys he left school at 15, before the "O" level examinations. But he has been having his suits custom-made since he was 12 at a place called Jackson's. He has his hair regularly cut in a College Boy by a hairdresser named Andy. All
– those – straight –
– noses up there have better jobs than he does, better addresses, they are nice old dads with manicured gardens out back and Austin 1100's, they have better accents, but he has … *The Life* … and a secret place he goes at lunchtime –
– a noonday underground.
Braaang – it is lunchtime. Why try to explain it to the straight noses? Larry Lynch puts this very straight look on his face, like a zombie mask, as if he were going to do the usual, go out and eat a good straight London lunch. All the straight human mummy-hubbies file on out for the standard London office-worker lunch. Boy! Off to the pubs to slop down the jowls with bitter and sandwiches with watercress stems in them. Or to Somebody's Chop House or Trattoria for the Big Time lunch, basting the big noonday belly and the big noon-day ego with Scotch salmon, French wine and coq au vin. Or a Small Time lunch in some place that looks like a Le Corbusier cathedral with white grotto plaster and jazz-organ stained glass, serving nice steaming hot sliced garden hose on buns. But – Larry – Lynch –
– with – his – straight mask on walks over to Shaftesbury Avenue and then almost to Tottenham Court Road, in the heart of the Oxford Street shopping district. The sun – the sun is out today – the sun shines off the glistening flaws on thousands of bursting lonely beetled faces on the sidewalk at noon, but Larry Lynch cuts in the doorway at 79 Oxford Street, a place called Tiles.
It is like suddenly turning off the light. The entryway is black, the stairs going down are black, black walls, black ceilings, winding around and around, like a maze, down into the blackness, until there is no daytime and no direction and suddenly –
– underground at noon –
– a vast black room heaving with music and human bodies. Up at one end is a small lighted bandstand. There is somebody up there at a big record turntable and rock music fills up the room like heavy water –
Bay-beh-eh
– and in the gloaming there are about 250 boys and girls, in

sexy kaks, you know, boys in codpiece pants, the age of codpiece pants, mini-skirts, mesh stockings, half-bras, tailored mons veneris, Cardin coats, navel-deep button-downs, Victoria shoes, inverted pleats, major hair, major eyes – eyes! – eyes painted up to here and down to there, with silver and gold beads just set in there like Christmas balls, set in the false eyelashes – all of them bucking about, doing the Spasm, the Hump, the Marcel, the Two-backed Beast in the blackness while a stray light from somewhere explodes on somebody's beaded eyelashes –

– down in the cellar at noon. Two hundred and fifty office boys, office girls, department store clerks, messengers, members of London's vast child work-force of teenagers who leave school at 15, pour down into this cellar, Tiles, in the middle of the day for a break … back into *The Life*. The man on the stage playing the records is Clem Dalton, a disc jockey. Off to one side in the dimness is a soft-drink stand, a beauty parlor called Face Place and an arcade of boutiques, a Ravel shoe store, a record shop, a couple of other places, all known as Tiles Street. There is a sign out there in the arcade that says Tiles Street, W1. The place is set up as an underground city for The Life.

Right away the music is all over you like a Vibro-Massage – and – Larry Lynch just starts waffling out onto the floor by himself – so what? – who needs a partner? – a lot of boys and girls come here at lunchtime and go into this kinetic trance, dancing by themselves, just letting the music grab them and mess up their minds. Berry Slee, a 19-year-old fellow from Brixton, is out there, in the darkness at noon, heh, going like a maniac, doing a dance called Rudy, by himself, with this maniacal suit on, with flaps on the pockets hanging down about eight inches, messes your mind right up, and Berry's friend, Ian Holton, who is also 19, is dancing by himself, too, and god, this *green* suit he has on, it *messes your mind up*, this waistcoat with the six buttons grouped in groups of two, great green groupy work by the great Jackson, like, one means, you know, the girls are all down here, too, but so what, the point is not making it with girls, there are plenty of girls out here dancing by themselves, too, the point is simply immersing yourself for one hour in The Life, every lunch hour.

Linda McCarthy from the Ravel store is out here, dancing with some guy, ratcheting her hips about in their sockets. Linda, with … The Eyes, is about to make it, as a model or something, it could happen, but just now she is 17 and she works in the Ravel shop and one moment she sells a pair of jesuschristyellow shoes and then the music gets her like a Vibro-Massage and she leaves the store and she goes out there and dances it out and then comes back, to the store, sell-a-shoe, and Jane Dejong is out there doing that, god, maniacal thigh-swivel dance she does. One knows? And Liz White and Jasmyn Hardwick, Chris Gray, John Atkinson, Jay Langford, a 15-year-old American kid, from Los Angeles, only he is really English now, from Willesden, and Steve Bashor, who lives down on the Strand, and is 17 but looks about 21, and he has already been to sea, in the Merchant Navy, and come back and now every day, in the dark, at noon he comes down into Tiles and stands on the edge of the bandstand and watches, he doesn't dance, he just watches and lets … the whole thing just take hold of him like the great god Vibro-Massage, and Sunshine Newman – oh god, Sunshine lost his job in the stationer's on Wardour Street but who gives a damn about that and Sunshine is going wild with some kind of yellow goggles on and his white turnover-neck jersey on, a checked jacket, sexy kaks. Who – cares – about

– the – sack – in –

– the – Noonday – Underground. Tiles has the usual "beat club" sessions on at night, with name groups up on the bandstand, and it packs them in, like a lot of other places, the Marquee, the Flamingo, the Ramjam, the Locarno Ballroom and so forth. But it is the lunchtime scene at Tiles, the noon-day underground, that is the perfect microcosm of The Life of working-class teenagers in England.

The thing is, The Life – the "mod" style of life that got going about 1960 – has changed within the last year. It has become a life of total – well, these kids have found a way to drop out almost totally from the conventional class-job system into a world they control. Practically all of them leave school at 15, so why do that old-style thing? Why live at home until you are 20 or 21, putting up with it all, having your manic sprees only on the weekends, having Mod and Rocker set-tos in the springtime or just messing up your mind on Saturday night at some dance hall.

Over the past year thousands of these working-class mods have begun moving away from home at 16, 17, or 18, even girls, girls especially, in fact, and into, flats in London. They go to work in offices, shops, department stores, for £8 to £10 a week, but that is enough to get them into The Life. They share flats, three, four, five girls to a flat, in areas like Leicester Square – Jaysus,

Leicester Square – Charing Cross, Charlotte Street, or they live with their boyfriends, or everyone drifts from place to place. Anyway, it all goes on within a very set style of life, based largely on clothes, music, hair-dos and a … super-cool outlook on the world.

It is the style of life that makes them unique, not money, power, position, talent, intelligence. So like most people who base their lives on style, they are rather gloriously unaffected cynics about everything else. They have far less nationalistic spirit, for example, than the orthodox English left-wing intellectual. They simply accept England as a country on the way down, and who gives a damn, and America as a country with the power, money, and if you can get some, fine, and the music is good, and you can get that, and they couldn't care less about Vietnam, war, the Bomb, and all that, except that English Army uniforms are indescribably creepy.

Their clothes have come to symbolize their independence from the old idea of a life based on a succession of jobs. The hell with that. There is hardly a kid in all of England who harbors any sincere hope of advancing himself in any very striking way by success at work. Englishmen at an early age begin to sense that the fix is in, and all that work does is keep you afloat at the place you were born into. So working-class teenagers, they are just dropping out of the goddam system, out of the job system, and into roles, as … Knights of the Codpiece Pants and Molls of the Mini Mons … The Life.

And nobody is even lapsing into the old pub system either, that business where you work your gourds off all day and then sink into the foamy quicksand of the freaking public house at night, loading up your jowls and the saggy tissues of your body with the foaming ooze of it all. Hell, one thing working-class teenagers know is that for five shillings, there is no way you can get drunk in the pub, but for five shillings you can buy enough pills – "purple hearts," "depth bombs" and other lovelies of the pharmacological arts – or "hash" or marijuana – Oh crazy Cannabis! – to stay high for hours. Not that anybody is turning on at Tiles in the noonday underground, but among working-class teenagers generally, in The Life, even the highs are different. The hell with bitter, watercress and old Lardbelly telling you it's time.

All that money, sodden with oozing foam, can better go into clothes. Practically all working-class teenagers in The Life devote half their pay, four to five pounds, to clothes. Some just automatically hand it over to their tailor each week because they always have him making something. There is no more contest between "mod" and "rocker" styles. The mod style and style of life have won completely. Working-class boys who do not dress in current mod styles – and they require a lot of money and, usually, a tailor – are out of it. Just like – shortly after Larry Lynch goes out there onto the dance floor, down into Tiles comes a 17-year-old kid wearing a non-mod outfit, a boho outfit, actually a pair of faded Levi's and a jacket cut like a short denim jacket, only made of suede, and with his hair long all around after the mode of the Rolling Stones, and he talks to a couple of girls on the edge of the dance floor and he comes away laughing and talking to some American who is down there.

"Do you know what she said to me?" he says. "She said, 'Sod off, Scruffy 'erbert.' They all go for a guy in a purple mohair suit. That's what they call me, 'Scruffy 'erbert.'"

"What's your name?"

"Sebastian."

He turns out to be Sebastian Keep, who works in London as a photographer's assistant but comes from a wealthy family in Hastings. He comes down into Tiles from time to time during his lunch hour to see Pat Cockell, who is 19 and runs the Ravel store in Tiles. Both of them are from Hastings and at one time or another attended public schools and the hell with all that, but on the other hand they illustrate the class split that persists, even in the world of London teenagers.

All the articles about "Swinging London" seem to assume that the class system is breaking down and all these great vital young proles from the East End are taking over and if you can get into Dolly's, Sibylla's, or David Bailey's studio you can see it happening. Actually, the whole "with-it" "switched-on" set of young Londoners – or the "New Boy Network," as it is called, as distinct from the Eton-Harrow "Old Boy Network" – is almost totally removed from the working-class mods. It is made up chiefly of bourgeois, occasionally better, but mainly bourgeois young men and women in the commercial crafts, photography, fashion, show business, advertising, journalism. Aside from the four Beatles themselves and, possibly, two actors, Terence Stamp and Michael Caine, and two photographers, David Bailey and Terence Donovan, there are no working-class boys in the New Boy Network.

The New Boys, including a few upper-class adventurers and

voyeurs, have borrowed heavily from the working-class mods in their style of life, but in a self-conscious way. Sebastian Keep's occupation, photographer's assistant, and his style of dress, 1964 Rolling Stones, are okay in the New Boy world. The suede jacket – cut and piped to look like a cotton denim pattern – cost 25 guineas, and this kind of reverse twist, like lining a raincoat with sable, is appreciated by the New Boys but to the mods – well, 25 guineas is a hell of a mohair suit at Jackson's, with the lapels cut like so, like a military tunic, you know? and – yes.

Only the New Boys, the bourgeois, turn up to buy clothes in London's male fashion centre, King's Road, in Chelsea. Both, the New Boys and the Mods, turn up in Carnaby Street, but more often the mods browse Carnaby Street like some kind of show place, or ambience, and then go off and have clothes like that made somewhere else, where it is cheaper, even a big chain outfit like Burton's.

Browsing Carnaby Street! God, before there was Tiles, that was what Sunshine used to do every day at lunch. Sunshine, whose real name is Tony Newman, of Stamford Hill, Tottenham, and who used to be called Blossom – well, Sunshine tops Blossom anyway – Sunshine would cut out of the stationer's store with the straight lunch mask on and then head straight for Carnaby Street and then just walk up and down Carnaby Street's weird two blocks for an hour, past the Lord John, Male West One, the Tom Cat, men's boutiques with strange enormous blown-up photographs in the windows, of young men flying through the air with some kind of Batman jockstraps on and rock music pouring out the doors, and kids just like him, Sunshine, promenading up and down, and tourists, christ, hundreds of tourists coming in there to photograph each other in front of Male West One instead of Big Ben, and busloads of schoolgirls with their green blazers on and embroidered crests on the breast pocket, all come to see the incredible Carnaby Street, which turns out to be a very small street with shops and awnings and people standing around with cameras in their hands, and Sunshines, all the Sunshines of this world, trundling up and down for their whole lunch hours not eating a goddamned thing, just immersing themselves in The Life.

That was before Tiles. On Saturday nights in Tiles there is an all-night session with kids stroked out from exhaustion on the steps at the far end of the arcade and then they revive and struggle upright again and jerk and buck a little in a comatose awakening and then they are awake and back out on the dance floor. It is like the Sisters in white dancing, by themselves, to the shout band at the funeral of Daddy Grace in Washington, D.C., going into that ecstatic kinetic trance, oh sweet Daddy, oh big bamboo, dancing until they dropped, and then they were dragged off to the side, prostrate, and they stayed that way until their heads started twitching and then they got up again, those mountains of devout fat got to writhing again.

On Whitsun weekend Tiles goes all day and all night and everybody gets a glimpse of the Total Life, the day when they can all really live completely, all day long, in a world of mod style, drenched in music, suited up, flipped out whipped, flayed, afire, melded, living a role – Knights of the Codpiece Pants. Molls of the Mini Mons – rather than a job. The whole idea of working-class or this class or that class will be irrelevant, except that –

– oh god, if only you could somehow make money without leaving The Life at all, the way Clem Dalton does, being a DJ, playing the records at Tiles, coming on with some swift American-style talk, having these great *performers* hanging around all the time, like Lee Curtis who sings at these American clubs in Germany, and Lyn Wolseley, who used to be with the Beat Girls and is a great dancer and everything. A DJ! So all these boys want to be DJs and they will do anything for a break.

Like Sunshine – one of Sunshine's big fears is that he is going to get stuck on another job like the one at the stationer's where he has to wear a necktie, because the thing is, Sunshine has developed his own variation within the mod style, which depends on wearing turnover-neck jerseys with these great tailored jackets, well – you know – a *white* turnover-neck can look great, practically formal.

Anyway, Sunshine went to Kenny Everett, who used to run the noontime sessions at Tiles. Kenny is also a DJ, and Sunshine wanted to get a job as a DJ at Radio Caroline or Radio Luxembourg, one of the pirate stations. It would be great, Sunshine heading out from shore for the first day, up in the front of a small boat, with his head up and the wind glancing off his yellow goggles, and his turnover-neck jersey, a red one, perhaps, up high, and his hands in his pockets. So Kenny Everett told him to make a tape and he would see what he could do for him. He told him just to come on with some patter like he was introducing a record, just some light patter, movement, not regular gags or anything.

So Sunshine got hold of a tape recorder and then the day came when he got in his room and held up the microphone of the tape recorder and then he concentrated on – what the hell is it these DJs say? – where does all that stuff come from? – and he could hear the voices of the DJs in his mind, all that stuff they say, things like, "Now, baby, one for the kidney machine, I mean one coming your way for the kidney machine, all those guys and gals down at the North College of Art, they're having their contest to raise money for the kidney machine, and Elise Thredder, down there at the college, you know what you wrote me about Cilla Black, Elise, you said I said she said we said they said oh my head, my head is – zowee! – now listen, Elise, I dig her, I dig her, I dig that girl, I'm telling you that, I've told you that, I dig her, dig her, and I dig all those police cadets, I mean it, and this one's for the kidney machine and the police cadets, coming your way, and I'm sorry, if anybody catches me with my hand in the shop window, remember, I played this one for the police cadets, and the kidney machine, and club members everywhere, bless their little hearts, their lih-uhl 'earts and their lih-uhl livers and their lih-uhl kidneys, no, I'm serious, ladies and gentlemen, and friends … I'm serious about this kidney machine, these gals at North College of Art are undertaking a most commendable endeavor, endeavoring to commendabobble the undertaker, you might say, in behalf of all those wonderful people with the – no – I mean that – and we're nothing until we're put to the test on the mountainside, and here it is, Mr. Billy Walker, and … *A Little on the Lonely Side.*"

How do they do it! So Sunshine does it. But he plays it back and it doesn't come out right somehow, he doesn't know exactly why, so he hasn't given it to Kenny yet, but someday, one day –

– one day Sunshine, and everybody, must find a way to break through the way Linda has. Oh god, Clem Dalton is the idol of the boys, they all want to be DJs, but Linda, who works in the shoe store, is practically the idol of the girls. Linda is on the verge of making it, of breaking through, making a living totally within The Life, and she is only 17.

Linda is a girl from Grays, in Essex. She left school at 15, like most of her six brothers and sisters, but they stayed in Grays, mostly, at home, until they grew up, but Linda, it is not that she is a wild girl or anything, it is just that … The Life, she was in it before she knew it. She could dance, and the way she wore her clothes – Linda doesn't have a skirt any lower than $7\frac{1}{2}$ inches above the knees, that is the truth, and these great bell-bottomed trousers, and her eyes, well, she paints on these incredible eyes, a big band of shadow, it looks an inch wide, between the upper lid and the eyebrows, then a black rim underneath and then she paints on eyelashes, paints them on, under her eyes, with these stripes reaching in picket rows down to her cheekbones, and her black bangs in front come down and just seem to be part of some incredible design ensemble with her eyes, it is all a pattern, a mask – anyway, Linda moved to London when she was 15, and she and three other girls moved into a flat on the motherless Leicester Square and pretty soon Linda was completely within The Life.

She took a job as a clerk, but it was, like – you know? – a total drag, and Linda started coming down to Tiles at noon, it was like a necessity, to get into The Life at midday before she flipped out in that flunky clerk world, and she was down there one day with her great face on, ratcheting her hips away, gone in the kinetic trance, and Pat Cockell saw her. He needed somebody, a girl, to come work in the Ravel shop in the arcade, somebody who would comprehend what all these working-class mod girls wanted when they came in. So he asked her.

Linda walked down the arcade and into the shops, and even in there, in through the door, she could hear the music from the bandstand. She could hear the music and the dance floor and all those kids would be about 50 feet away, that was all, and it would be like almost being in The Life all the time. So she took the job and pretty soon she would be selling a shoe and then nobody is in the shop for a moment, so Pat stays in there and she goes out to the dance floor and gets into the kinetic trance for one number and then comes back and sells some girl a jesuschristyellow pair of shoes.

Linda was making £9 10s a week. About 25 shillings went to taxes, £2 as her share of the flat, £3 or £4 a week to clothes, at places like Biba – and 30 shillings a week for food. That's all! Thirty shillings – but god, look, she looks great, and what are all these regular straight three-a-day *food injections* for, anyway. And then one day Linda was selling a pair of jesuschristyellow shoes or something and then ratcheting about on the Tiles dance floor and somebody told Marjorie Proops, the columnist, about her, and she ran her picture and then Desilu Productions, the TV company, was doing something about London and they put her in a scene, and now these photographers come by and take her picture – and Linda is *on the verge*, she could become a model or … a *figure*, a celebrity, however these things happen, with Pat

Cockell as her manager, oh god, Linda could make it, living The Life totally … and yet Linda doesn't really give all that much of a damn about it.

People come in and talk to Linda, like this American who was in there, and she listens and she answers questions, but then Clem Dalton puts on something out there, like *Hideaway* –

Hideaway … Come on! … far from the light of day … Come on! … leaving the world behind.

– and Linda's eyes kind of glaze over and her legs, in the pinstripe bell-bottoms, start pumping and then she is out the door and out into the dark, at noon, in Tiles. *That's where we're gonna stay.* And so what if she doesn't make it. The Life is still there, it is still available for less than £10 a week, Clem Dalton will never forsake, Jackson will live forever, *I-love-you drops, I-miss-you drops*, and Ian Holton will be abroad in the streets of London with a green waistcoat on that messes your mind up, and Berry Slee and Jay, Liz, Jasmyn, Jane, all the Jays, Lizzes, Jasmyns, Janes of this world – and Larry Lynch –

Hideaway – Larry Lynch looks down at his wrist, beautiful the way that cuff just sort of wells out, white, out of the checked sleeve, a half inch of beautiful Brixton cuff, debouching, and Christ, he is already twelve minutes over, and he heads back through the maze of Tiles, through the black, like unwinding himself, and up the black stairs – volt! – the sun hits him and nearly tears his eyes out, but the same bursting beetled faces are still bobbing and floating past on the sidewalks and the same shops, hacks, cops, the same Marks & Spencer … the same Leicester Square and – oh splendid – he knew it would be this way, there, back in the office, even, even, straight, straight, the same rows of … straight noses, all pointing the same way, toward eternity, as if nothing had happened at all.

11 QUANT ON QUANT – MARY QUANT

Early Modernist fashions were not too kind to girls and although Quant came to represent the Chelsea set, she was still a vital player in and for the Modernists.

Once only the rich, the Establishment, set the fashion. Now it is the inexpensive little dress seen on the girls in the High Street. These girls may have their faults. Often they may be too opinionated and extravagant. But the important thing is that they are alive ... looking, listening, ready to try anything new.

It is their questioning attitude which makes them important and different. They conform to their own set of values but not to the values and standards laid down by a past generation. But they don't sneer at other points of view. If they don't wish to campaign against the Bomb, they don't sneer at those who do. They are not silly or flirtatious or militant. Being militant and aggressive is as ridiculous to them as being coy and deliberately seductive. They make no pretensions.

Sex is taken for granted. They talk candidly about everything from puberty to homosexuality. The girls are curiously feminine but their femininity lies in their attitude rather than in their appearance. They may be dukes' daughters, doctors' daughters or dockers' daughters. They are not interested in status symbols. They don't worry about accents or class; they are neither determinedly county nor working-class. They are scornful of pretence of any kind.

There was a time when clothes were a sure sign of a woman's social position and income group. Not now. Snobbery has gone out of fashion, and in our shops you will find duchesses jostling with typists to buy the same dresses.

Once upon a time if two women turned up at a party wearing the same dress, it wrecked the party. There were hysterical outbursts and one of them probably walked out. Nowadays, it is not unusual to see several identical dresses at the same party and the girls love it. You can see them huddling together, delighted at this confirmation of their own good taste. At Washington's Opera Ball this year, I believe there were fifteen or twenty identical or indistinguishable dresses and the hostess, the French Ambassador's wife, Mme Hervé Alpand, said she thought it gave 'a kick to the ball – in a nice way, of course'.

The voices, rules and culture of this generation are as different from those of the past as tea and wine. And the clothes they choose evoke their lives …. daring and gay, never dull.

They think for themselves. They are committed and involved. Prejudices no longer exist. They represent the whole new spirit that is present-day Britain, a classless spirit that has grown out of the Second World War.

They will not accept truisms or propaganda. They are superbly international. The same clothes are worn in Britain, Europe and America. The same sort of food is eaten, too. I think there may be a chance that you can't swing a war on a generation which does not think in terms of 'us' against the foreigners.

The young will not be dictated to. You can be publicised on the national network television programmes, be written up by the most famous of the fashion columnists and the garment still won't sell if the young don't like it.

I admire them tremendously.

These girls may start as the ones who fill the coffee bars in worn jeans, dirty duffle coats and with uncombed hair but they can change – almost overnight. They are the Mods. At first glance the uninitiated may find it hard to tell the sexes apart. The traditional symbols have gone. Brilliant colour is today as permissible in men's wear as it is in as women's. Long and short hair cuts are worn by both. Since the sexes live much the same sort of lives, they want the same sort of clothes to live them in.

It is the Mods … the direct opposite of the Rockers (who seem to be anti-everything) … who gave the dress trade the impetus to break through the fast-moving, breathtaking, up-rooting revolution in which we have played a part since the opening of Bazaar.

We had to keep up with them. We had to expand.

12 THE YOUNG METEORS – JONATHAN AITKEN

Before his reign as a Conservative cabinet minister, Aitken worked as a journalist in the '60s covering the young meteors, as his 1967 book was called. These included Barbara Hulanicki at Biba and street Mods obsessed with clothes.

A boutique can be defined as a small shop of flamboyant atmosphere specialising in original and colourful clothes, usually at prices. There are an estimated 2,000 of them in Greater London, and apart from John Stephen's chain of men's boutiques, virtually all are run by small-time entrepreneurs, often part-time designers themselves. The classic boutique is perhaps Biba's in Kensington Church Street, where an estimated 3,000 dolly birds each week push through the hearty Victorian wood and brass doors, intent on dissipating their last shillings on the tempting sartorial baubles of the Aladdin's cave that lies within. Amidst the Victorian splendour of a massive panoply of burgundy-coloured mock flock wallpaper and heavy mahogany wardrobes, all the flamboyance of the swinging fashion cult stands exposed. Everything from luminous pink socks to sombrero-sized felt hats and pop art jewellery is here in colourful profusion, and while all boutiques cater for the mini-skirt, this one's strength is that it also caters for the mini budget. The most expensive items in Biba's cost around £7, while the average price of a dress runs only to £2.10.0. and many garments and accessories can be picked up for only a few shillings.

The owner is 29-year-old former fashion artist Barbara Hulanicki (she named the shop after her sister Biba), who came to London from Jerusalem in 1948, and started her career in the rag trade three years ago selling a few dresses by mail order from her flat.

> We try to keep everything as cheap as possible, about half the price of anything everywhere else. We do all the designing and manufacturing ourselves to keep the mark-up low, and because we're big by boutique standards we can stock up to five hundred of each design.

Biba's customers, although including many celebrity names such as Brigitte Bardot, Julie Christie, Françoise Hardy, Baroness von Thyssen and Mia Farrow, are virtually all working girls of slender £10-£15 weekly incomes. Yet despite these comparatively meagre resources Miss Hulanicki calculates that the average Biba's shopper spends between £6 and £7 a week on clothes and accessories. The high expenditure rate never ebbs since "after a month's wear a new dress is an antique" and the worst economic freeze does not touch the pockets of secretaries.

I interviewed several typical-looking customers as they emerged from Biba's one Saturday afternoon:

> I spend about £8 here each week – it's my weakness, I suppose. Yes, it is a lot considering I only earn £13, but then I save up all my luncheon vouchers and sell them off to the greedy boys in the office, sometimes my dad gives me a quid or two when he's had a good night at the dogs, and sometimes I get something off my boy-friend as a present.

> I couldn't afford to buy any clothes at all on my salary as a secretary after paying the rent and all that. But I do three nights a week as a waitress, and this brings me in about six quid clothes money. It's worth it to look good the other four nights.

> I love clothes. They're to me what drink and drugs are to other people. I like them because it's a way of advertising myself to men. I spend about half my wages here. If I've done overtime and haven't had to waste any cash on taxis, I should have about £6 to spare. Frankly though, if I come here and I see something I really like

and can't quite afford it, I just nick it.

This, apparently, is no idle boast. Shoplifting is the scourge of the rag trade, and the Aladdin's cave of Biba's has a constant struggle to prevent itself from becoming the more notorious cavern of Ali Baba and the Forty Thieves. Says Miss Hulanicki:

> It's the worst of our problems. On our opening day we lost one hundred and three pairs of ear-rings, seventy-eight pairs of sunglasses and God knows what else. That was just the opening! Now we've got quite good precautions, and we prosecute on an average between seven and twelve people a week. You have to prosecute every one you catch because if you don't, the word whistles round that Biba's lets you off, and then they bring all their little sisters and little brothers to join in the game. Some of these innocent-looking little birds are absolutely ruthless thieves – you'd be astonished.

Despite the shop lifting, Biba's is reputed to have the highest turnover per square foot of any store in the world, including Marks & Spencer and Nieman-Marcus. At times the atmosphere resembles Piccadilly Circus at rush hour, and shoppers have to pile in three and four to a fitting cubicle, a situation which is exacerbated when, as often happens, one of the girls brings her steady boy-friend into the cubicle to assist with the fit. But all this no doubt adds to the excitement, and for all its excesses Biba's must unquestionably be awarded top rating for its style…

…The other great boutique centre is Carnaby Street, a frenzied pulsating two block alley-way behind Regent Street, where the video-aural jazzle of pop sounds and op colours will send even the soberest of minds into a temporary LSD-style vision. It is the concentration of Carnaby Street that provides the flavour, for there is only two hundred and fifty yards of it, yet every inch bursts with super-clothes in super-colour and the effect is riotous.

On a Saturday morning the crowds, all in their teens or very early twenties, get so thick that the jostle is positively sensual, adding the erotic to the exotic. Here is the weekly Ascot for the mods and dolly birds, who dress for the occasion as carefully as any deb or debs' delight bound for the Royal enclosure. A few comments from Carnaby Street:

Yes, sure I come here every week. From Birmingham, in fact. Well, I do have to get up at six in the morning, which is two hours earlier than I normally do, but then my clobber matters to me whereas my work matters only to my boss. I always buy something that's new in style, the very latest. In Brum I've got quite a name for being well-dressed. At home I've got over seventy pairs of trousers and twenty jackets. Mauve is my favourite colour, I'm famous for my mauve. I spend about £7 each week here but if the piece-work has been really good I could spend more. The most I ever spent was £23, that was after I won the bingo competition.

I come here just to be part of the scene. I never actually buy anything myself, although Pam does. [Pam was his bird, dressed in orange tights, six inches of naked stomach, and a silver sequined top.] Carnaby Street gear is so badly made to my way of thinking, so what I do is note down some of the good ideas for designs then when I get back home to Peckham I go round to a little shop round the corner where there's this little jew boy ever so sharp. He makes up my gear at cost price, then as he's got the designs he makes up a few jackets and sells them off as Peckham exclusives. Makes a bomb I bet.

Hi Mister! Dontyer want to interview me? I'm a king. I'm Martin of the Movetones. Haven't you heard of the Movetones? Well, if you lived in Poplar you would have done. We're the top group and I'm the lead guitarist. You should hear me playing the solo in Saturday Night at the Duckpond. No, goofy, it's a song not a pub. I suppose I make around £60 a week. I spend about £50 of it in Carnaby Street. No I'm not exaggerating. We artists get our clothes tax free, which is right since they build our image. I'm having a sequin jacket and trousers made now. Ordered it today. It'll cost me £80.

Carnaby Street today still packs in the swingers and mods up from the suburbs, but it is becoming somewhat over-self-consciously the land of American Express and Diners Club cards. Once a place is accepted on the tourists' map of the scene it is out for the real swingers. Today, it is mainly foreigners and outsiders who throng the street, but there are enough of them to keep business flowing.

13 THE POP PROCESS – RICHARD MABEY

Ready Steady Go on Friday night was the signal to start the Mod weekend. This piece gives you some good facts about the show and is followed up with Richard Barnes's take on it.

Of all the TV and radio pop programmes, Rediffusion's *Ready, Steady, Go!* on Friday evenings has, deservedly, the highest reputation. *R.S.G.*'s success has been due entirely to two unique features: live performances and a carefully chosen teenage audience. *R.S.G.* was the first television show to risk live appearances by top recording artists, and it was an initiative of which those shows that have kept to miming must be very jealous. It demolished finally the widespread myth that most singers could only make an acceptable noise with the help of recording-studio tricks. (A few groups have been conspicuously absent since *R.S.G.* went live, but the reasons for this may be quite unconnected.) The majority – and the Animals and Manfred Mann, in particular – have proved what anyone who has seen them perform in clubs or dance-halls knew all along: that they are far more exciting playing freely to a responsive audience (with all the loss of echo and effects that this may mean) than attempting to move their mouths in time with a record, which, after a hundred identical plays, has lost all meaning for them.

   Ready, Steady, Go's choice of music is wide and progressive, and it never confines itself to the safe favourites of *Juke Box Jury* and *Thank Your Lucky Stars* (though it does tend to pander to London modishness).

It has presented distinguished blues artists like John Lee Hooker and Jesse Fuller, and folksingers like Buffy St Marie, Paul Simon and Donovan when the latter was still a scruffy lad just up from St. Ives. And one memorable Friday – it must be the only occasion on record when the dancing stopped completely – Paul Jones of the Manfred Mann group was allowed to sing "With God on Our Side," Bob Dylan's biting anti-war song that the B.B.C. had unofficially banned.

R.S.G.'s audience are mostly teenagers from London clubs, and to be admitted to the programme they have to pass a short dancing audition. The producers presumably feel that the subsequent loss of spontaneity is a small price to pay for the stylish, fast-moving character which they give the programme. For, in spite of a tendency to become giggly and exhibitionist when they see the cameras near them, they are mostly very good dancers indeed. (Like the faithful troupe of shouters who follow Geno Washington's Ram Jam Bands they are more extensions of the groups than members of an audience.) In fact, for anyone who finds live musical performances as exciting to watch as they are to listen to, R.S.G. is a visual goldmine: cameras swooping back and forth like robot jivers, tangled black leads from the guitars, and Pop Art decor. Admittedly, all of these serve to exaggerate the excitement of the music. But they are more an integral part of pop than the equivalent accoutrements at a serious concert are of classical music. R.S.G. is much talked about by teenagers, particularly outside London, where it is one of the few channels through which knowledge of the latest fashions can be obtained: the viewers know where those dancers are chosen from. But it is precisely in an arrogant awareness of this fashionable reputation that the programme's main weakness lies. The hostess, Cathy McGowan, for all her disarming artlessness and powder-room chatter, is constantly dictating what is, is not, and will be 'in'. There was once a ritual in which one of the visiting stars would wander round the audience and pick out the girl he would most like to go out with. Not that she ever got a date, of course. Her rewards were usually a peck on the cheek and a free L.P. How one wished that, just once, the star or his luckless choice would refuse to collaborate in this embarrassing and rather cruel charade.

14   MODS – RICHARD BARNES

Ready Steady Go! would fly acts over from the States. It was
worth it for a lot of American artists to visit England to do
R.S.G. because they were bigger in England than they were in
the States. I remember seeing Jimmy Reed once at the Flamingo.
He didn't have any idea what was going on. There he was, trying
to make his living out of putting his suffering to music, and
suddenly he's flown out of his country to Europe to play to rich
white kids all pilled out of their minds and treating him like the
Messiah. He was standing there playing his guitar looking very
bewildered, with his manager next to him, both still in their
overcoats and scarves.

   R.S.G. had a number of specials too. They had a Beatles
special, and a Stones special, one for the Who and I think one
for Otis Redding or James Brown. The London based bands
became almost regulars, such as The Who, Animals and Stones.
People like Mick Jagger and Kenny Lynch always happened to
be passing by and would pop in.

   Not only did *R.S.G.* keep Mods up to date on dances, but it
also had on some of the best-dressed Mods every week, so the
rest of the country saw something of London Mods' clothes.
Some kids were very influenced by the fashions they saw on
R.S.G.. Paul Beecham was one of the dancers from the scene
who was regularly on the programme. It is said that he was one
of the originators of the 'Block'. He used to appear wearing
jeans with small turn-ups, hockey-boots with the studs removed,
and a cycling shirt. He was on for six weeks and then was ill. A
couple of weeks later while still ill he watched the show and saw

a kid dancing in exactly the same clothes he'd worn. 'The guy even copied my watch-strap and the way I wore my watch with the face on the inside of the wrist.'

Johnny Moke recalls one particular show 'Sandie Shaw was on the show and it was her first T.V. appearance. She had to walk along a bit and go up three steps. She couldn't see very well without her glasses, so somebody, I think it was one of the technicians, suggested she took her shoes off and felt along the cable with her feet up to the steps. She did and got known for being the barefoot singer.'

The signature tune opening *R.S.G.* was a current hit from the time and was changed about every six months. The most apt was *Anyway, Anyhow, Anywhere* by the Who. The record has always seemed to me to be about a typical 'pilled up' Mod. It might not, I've never heard Pete Townshend talk about the song. It could just as easily be about his new found wealth or the state of his ego at that time.

> *I can go anyway, way I choose,*
> *I can live anyhow, win or lose,*
> *I can go anywhere for something new,*
> *Anywhere, anyhow, anyway I choose.*
> *I can do anything, right or wrong;*
> *I can talk anyhow to get along.*
> *I don't care anyway, I never lose,*
> *Anyway, anyhow, anywhere I choose.*

The two essentials that a full time Soho Mod needed in the Sixties to keep him on the go were money and energy. Most Mods were in a clean clerical job that was relatively well paid. There wasn't a large unemployment problem for school leavers then. If they didn't have the money they wouldn't try to be in the competitive top league. They would improvise and get by. I know of kids that would stay indoors for weeks until they'd saved enough to buy whatever it was that they found they weren't able to live without. Rather than be seen not looking right, it was better not to be seen.

In order to keep up the hectic pace that was expected of the true Mod, he would have to supplement his energy. The true Mod was half real and half myth. The itinerary of our ideal Mod went like this. Monday evening The Scene Club. Tuesday local dance. Wednesday, La Discotheque. Thursday, The Scene again or maybe the Marquee or the Lyceum. Friday, *Ready, Steady,*

Go! and then on to the Scene or La Discotheque. Saturday, shopping down Carnaby Street in the morning, then to Imhoffs or some obscure record shop in Hampstead or Brixton. Saturday night to the Flamingo and Allnighter. Leave the Allnighter at four in the morning and go to a Sunday morning street-market like Petticoat Lane or Brick Lane for tea and breakfast and to browse among the record and clothes stalls. Sunday afternoon back to the Flamingo for the afternoon session. Sunday evening to the Crawdaddy club in Richmond, ending up for a cappuccino at L'Auberge coffee bar by Richmond Bridge until midnight.

Somewhere in all that he'd have to fit in washing his hair and a little time to listen to the records he'd bought. Even if this was the Mod myth, many Mods kept up a lifestyle almost as hectic as this. Most were broke by Monday morning but could still keep going. Johnny Moke: 'All you needed was about 1/- for fares, 6d there and 6d back. It was two bob to get in the Lyceum or Tottenham Royal. I didn't drink or smoke, I might buy an orange drink which was 6d. All we wanted to do was dance.'

15   THE LAMBERTS – ANDREW MOTION

For many years The Who were regarded as the *Mod band. This extract finally puts that notion to waste and, as we will discover later, sets the ground for the tragic rise and fall of Pete Meaden, the man who brought Mod and The Who to the masses and then couldn't get into the show.*

As an art student, Townshend was quite simply resented by other members of the band. Although they respected his talent and valued the support of his family, they envied and distrusted the articulacy that his intelligence and education gave him. Entwistle, because he was a comparatively old and trusting friend of Townshend's was prepared to accept this. To Daltrey, it constituted a threat. The lead singer Colin Dawson felt the same, and so did the drummer Daltrey had enlisted, Doug Sandom, who was generally agreed to be, musically speaking, 'ten times better than we were'. To start with these conflicts were either overwhelmed by the group's collective desire to make their mark – they quickly established themselves as a popular club band in the Shepherd's Bush area – or rerouted into dissatisfaction with the singer, Dawson. 'He didn't fit,' says Sandom. 'I mean, Peter hated to see a singer like he was. He'd just stand there and wiggle his bum.' The solution to the problem was in one respect decisive – Dawson was sacked – and in another muddled: the singing was shared between Daltrey and an ex-member of The Bel-Aires called Gabby. Daltrey, as Marsh says, was nobody's idea of a subtle song stylist, and the only advantage of this revised line up was to give the five-man Detours a sound which at least made them different from the very large number of four-man groups which dominated rock and roll in the early 1960s. It also, however, prevented them from establishing a proper coherence. They argued, relied heavily on other bands' songs for their material – especially Beatles' songs and Motown numbers – and presented their audience with a fragmented image.

Their audience did not care much since by luck as well as judgment The Detours had managed to attract a following which was simply hungry for a band to speak for them. One of their most regular venues was the Goldhawk Social Club in the Goldhawk Road connecting Shepherd's Bush with Chiswick, later to be institutionalised as a favourite stamping ground for Mods, but in its early days a haunt for virtually any kind of angry young man. 'The guys in there,' one of the Club's members recalls, 'weren't Mods or Rockers. They were loners ... [It was] packed with guys who were just coming out of nick.' As English rock and roll became less dependent on America so different kinds of music attracted more easily definable kinds of fans. Where the Rockers, for instance, elected to identify with the impression of squalor and threat cultivated by bands like The Rolling Stones, the Mods created a more stylish image for themselves. 'It was a true cult,' Marsh says, 'with almost religious overtones', and its aspirations were embodied in a code of behaviour which mingled the longing for novelty and independence with the realisation that the means of achieving these things could only be acquired by discipline and hard work. 'It was fashionable, it was clean and it was groovy. You could be a bank clerk and a Mod,' said Townshend.

This version of Mods – a suddenly coherent section of young England which was, in Daltrey's phrase, 'the first generation to have a lot of money after the war', and were using it to have good clean fun – is strikingly at odds with the original flavour of the Goldhawk Social Club. But the Mods' rebellion had a more threatening aspect too. 'The archetypal Mod,' said Nik Cohn, the rock and roll commentator and entrepreneur, 'was male, sixteen years old, rode a scooter, swallowed pep pills by the hundred, thought of women as a completely inferior race, was obsessed by cool and dug it. He was also one hundred per cent hung up on himself. On his clothes and hair and image; in every way, he was a miserable narcissistic little runt.'

It was this disruptiveness, mingled with a wish for self-advancement by orthodox means, which The Detours and their audience identified in each other. It did not take their first managers long to realise they could adapt their image to exploit the recognition. The managers were in fact no more than ambitious amateurs. Initially, Sandom's sister's boss, Hal Gorden (who ran a brass foundry), had tried to turn himself into a version of The Beatles' manager, Brian Epstein, by arranging various gigs, but he soon found that he needed help with promotion, and employed Pete Meaden, who had recently been sacked as one of The Rolling Stones' publicists for being 'a pigheaded Mod'.

Meaden quickly set about sharpening The Detours' image. The change most badly needed was exposed by a recording session he arranged in the spring of 1964 with Chris Parmeinter, who worked for Fontana Records. Parmeinter was impressed by The Detours, but told Meaden, 'If you want to make a record, you'll have to get the drumming sorted out.' The band, supported by Meaden, knew that the Mod audiences on which they depended might be quickly swept away on a new tide of fashion, and rounded on Sandom. He left within a week of the visit to Fontana, and his place was taken by a series of session drummers imported from other groups. In April, though, one of their gigs was interrupted by a drunk who told them he had a friend who could help them out. 'He brought up this little gingerbread man,' Entwistle remembers, 'dyed ginger hair, brown shirt, brown tie, brown suit, brown shoes … he got up on the kit and we said, "Can you play 'Roadrunner'?" 'cos we hadn't come across a drummer that could play "Roadrunner" with us. And he played it, and we thought, "Oh this is the fellow." He played it perfectly.' His name was Keith Moon, and he was enlisted at once…

… Moon completed the band's musical jigsaw, and his arrival coincided with the greatest success Meaden was to have as manager. In March 1964 – the month before Moon appeared – the Mods had become headline news when they went on the rampage at the Essex coastal resort of Clacton, on a Bank Holiday, and the bands with which they associated were accordingly thrust into prominence. Meaden had already experimented with ways of identifying The Detours more closely with their audience, considering changing their name to The Who before deciding on The High Numbers. (The Who is an old musical joke 'They're called The Who.' 'The Who?' 'The Who.', etc., etc.) Meaden also redesigned the band's clothing, dressing Daltrey as a 'face' and the others as 'tickets'. Pete later explained: 'These were like two phrases that we used ... "faces" were the leaders – they were very hard to find, very few. "Tickets" were the masses.' The phrase 'high numbers' was itself part of Mod parlance: to be a 'high number' was to be notably hip.

Townshend endorsed and elaborated the changes that Meaden made by suggesting various alterations of his own. Many were derived from ideas that he had come across at art school. He was particularly keen to find ways of performing which might express the same impatience with convention that fascinated him in the work of the 'autodestructive artist' Gustav Metzke, under whose spell he had recently fallen. (Metzke was notorious for the violence of his opinions and techniques. His working methods included painting in acid on metal.) To start with, Metzke's influence did little more than prompt the band to increase their volume, perform in a way which seemed bound to insult each other and the audience, and damage their instruments. Later, under Kit's management Metzke's example was translated into scenes of truly barbaric destructiveness. Like Meaden, Townshend was anxious to clarify the band's image to a point which stopped just short of alienating the record companies on whom their success depended. When, in June 1964, Parmeinter at Fontana realised that he could use The High Numbers to exploit the Mod market, the band eagerly submitted to the routine of recording in a studio.

During the first session at Fontana, The High Numbers recorded two R-and-B cover versions – Eddie Holland's Tamla hit "Leavin' Here", and Bo Diddley's "Here 'Tis". Because Meaden felt, according to Marsh, that they needed to make 'a clear statement of Mod principles', the songs were never released, and it was decided to record original material instead. Since no one in the band was yet writing songs, Meaden met the challenge by reworking two little-known American records, Slim Harpo's "Got Love if You Want It", which became "I'm The Face", and "Country Fool" by The Showmen, which became "Zoot Suit". They were released on 3 July 1964 with "I'm The Face" on the A side, were politely but quietly reviewed, struggled to find a lowly place in the charts (which that summer included The Beatles' "A Hard Day's Night", The Rolling Stones' "It's All Over Now", The Animals' "The House of The Rising Sun", and Manfred Mann's "Do Wah Diddy Diddy"), and vanished.

Not even the appearance in 1964 of the first pirate radio ships

– Radio Caroline began broadcasting in March, and Radio Atlantic in July – could create a market for The High Numbers. (However, the stations did radically affect sales of pop music generally: 613,000 singles were sold in England in 1963, 718,000 in 1964). Fontana, not surprisingly, showed no signs of wanting to issue a follow-up, Gorden and Meaden began to argue about how best to proceed, and the band themselves began to feel disaffected. The Beatles had managed to get rich quick. Why shouldn't The High Numbers?

16   SOMETHING BEGINNING WITH 'O' – KEVIN PEARCE

Kevin Pearce's manifesto on pop and culture, Something Beginning With 'O *deserved a far wider audience than it gained. Here he delves into the strange world of Mod groups and reports back with love and accuracy.*

"It was splendid, simply splendid, chaps, the way this boy would see the horses home before he laid a bet." – *Stevie Smith,* Novel On Yellow Paper

"The mods were, for me, the revolution, the revolutionary group, they're the VietCong out in Cambodia, you know? There's a North Vietnamese army who are stolid troops, and there's the VietCong who are like mods, who are the ones who've been fighting all the time. They've never let down the side, they've never come in strength, they've always been fighting in a minority group, against the vast armour of the American army." – *Pete Meaden*

As Mod went overground, the old originals looked on in horror at the lumpen latterday mods marauding around, jumping around to the sweat-soaked soul sounds of Jimmy James and the Vagabonds and Geno Washington and the Ram Jam Band.

Pete Meaden said that Jimmy James had the best voice ever. Meaden had a vested interest. Jimmy James and the Vagabonds were Meaden's second stab at monopolising the mod market. His first fling had been with The Who.

Way back Meaden believed that the underground mod

movement needed a focal point. He adopted a promising, directionless r'n'b group. He taught them to be mods. He dressed them up in authentic mod clothes, gave them all the right things. He wrote two authentic mod anthems for them on speed. He secured the Tuesday night Marquee residency for them, then lost out to businessmen when people started taking notice. He went back to basics with Jimmy James and the Vagabonds' homegrown hard driving purist mod r'n'b until nobody was taking notice.

The Who merely mimicked mods. The Small Faces were the real thing. They were the right size, and they came from the mod rank and file. They were fun, they were common and they were great pop stars, but there was no strangeness, no obsessiveness. Everybody knows about The Who and Small Faces, but there was much more to the mod uprising. There was My Degeneration as well as My Generation, The Eyes have it over the known. The Eyes had a sense of the absurd. They had dramatic discordant clanging guitars. They wore great customised shirts with evil eyes on, and sang strange songs about immediate pleasure and girls with grey suede coats and souls like fire.

The Creation were at the pop art experimental end of the mod market. "Our music is red – with purple flashes," said Eddie Phillips of The Creation. Eddie Phillips had a great haircut and the greatest guitar sound ever. He scraped his strings with a violin bow, and went in for free form feedback and abstract phrases.

The Creation played way-out pop, beaten up blues. Their first foray, Making Time, was upfront and urgent. The song was aggressive, argumentative, articulate: "Why do we have to carry on always singing the same old song?"

The Creation's live shows were non stop movement, climaxing with an action painting being ceremoniously set fire to. Antics on a par with The Flies pissing on the audience at the Alexandra Palace 14-Hour Technicolor Dream, two people onstage sitting on a sofa reading newspapers as Subway Sect played, Einsturzende Neubauten and accomplices setting about the ICA stage with pneumatic drills. In the '60s The Creation stayed strictly underground. They were pioneers, explorers, out on their own. The Creation released a string of great Shel Talmy-produced singles. In the '70s Punk Rock luminaries the Sex Pistols and The Jam covered Creation songs, and both Johnny Rotten and Paul Weller chose to play Creation songs on the radio. The Jam used a Creation single as part of the artful All

Mod Cons collage, but strangely MOR disco doyens Boney M had the huge hit with The Creation's new art school anthem, Painter Man: "Here was where the money lay. Classic art has had its day."

In the '80s, underground groups like the TV Personalities, Times and Biff Bang Pow! were obsessed by The Creation and astutely appropriated aspects of the '60s mod uprising and '70s Punk Rock explosion. It all fitted.

> "What you're talking about is a form of hard pop which may have been prevalent in the '60s, but if you were buying the right records around '77 to '79 you would've heard exactly that same kind of pop, that sensibility being put out under slightly different sounds. I mean, you're not going to tell me that The Clash aren't the same sensibility as The Creation, 'cos they are – it's noise and it's pop." – *Joe Foster, Creation Records, October 1984*

The Action were at the dandy, flash, foppish end of the mod market. When The Action came to town, all the local mods would turn out to give the group a ceremonial scootercade. Singer Reggie King had a great haircut and the greatest voice ever. He sang soul, so sweetly, so smoothly, with the occasional trace of a classless London accent. It was all strangely natural, never forced, everything flowed. The Action played the mods' own Motown sound with such panache that Berry Gordy sat up and applauded.

On Spector/Goffin/King's "Just Once in My Life", The Action effortlessly outstripped the Righteous Brothers in the blue eyed soul stakes, and The Action's own songs took the soul thing a little further, with dramatic natural harmonies and Rickenbacker tintinnabulation.

In the '60s The Action were the Great Unknowns. They released a string of great George Martin-produced singles. An Action LP was recorded and abandoned, though Rave ran a design The Action's LP cover competition. In the early '80s The Action found a whole new appreciative audience when the *Ultimate Action* compilation appeared with Weller's liner notes.

In the late '80s when a mother went to Erith Gollege, South London, on one of the government's adult training courses, she came across a strange little chap, a real swinging London gentleman dandy, who claimed that he sang with a group once.

One day at home she mentioned that his name was Reggie King. Her stunned son showed her the *Ultimate Action* sleeve. "My God, that is him," she said. "The hair, the suit, everything." The real Reggie King perfectly preserved. The looks, the voice, the figure. He may not be rich or recognised, but he has been the best. That is what matters.

Reggie King, who speaks the way that he sings, once said: "A while back I was at Dingwalls to see Dr Feelgood, this great new group with a mad guitarist with staring eyes, when Robert Plant came up to my table with his manager Grant and their entourage, and said: 'You're Reggie King. I used to go and see you all the time. You were the best.' I should have said: 'Invest some of your money in me then,' but I wouldn't lower myself. I've never pushed myself. I've always been too lazy."

The Action were at their best playing live, playing the latest stateside soul songs and their own creations. They toured with P.J. Proby and The Action's regular Marquee performances are more fondly remembered than The Who's. Even The Action's stark black and white Marquee posters were better than The Who's. There was one club in the North East called The Place that The Action were so fond of, they wrote a song about never going back there.

There is another Pete Jenner-produced LP, *The Action Speak Louder Than ...* it is not The Action. Reggie King is on the cover, but he is not singing. "I left and that was that, the end. A group cannot carry on without the singer." Without King to sing, The Action became Mighty Baby, all moustaches and psychedelic excess. Reggie King stayed on the soul side. He kept a low profile, and never let it down. He went to work with Giorgio Gomelsky, and released a solitary solo LP on United Artists in 1971, before disappearing from view.

After an almost fatal fall down a flight of stone steps, Reggie King was in and out of hospitals for years, with amnesia and all kinds of complications. Once recovered, he disappeared again into suburban anonymity, alone, strong enough to survive, maintaining the mystery.

> "Better hold on to those dreams baby
> That's all you've got you know, your dreams
> We all love you, all your friends
> Keep those dreams burning, forever
> Yeah, keep those flames glowing man."
> – Suicide, "Dreams"

17 HOMEGROWN COOL: THE STYLE OF THE MODS – DICK HEBDIGE

Dick Hebdige's book, Subculture and the Meaning of Style, *is an academic look at youth and fashion. This extract makes some pertinent points about Modernism, not least its refusal to indulge in silly minded racism.*

By the early 60s, however, sizeable immigrant communities had been established in Britain's working-class areas, and some kind of rapport between blacks and neighbouring white groups had become possible.

The mods were the first in a long line of working-class youth cultures which grew up around the West Indians, responded positively to their presence and sought to emulate their style. Like the American hipster described above, the mod was a 'typical lower-class dandy' (Goldman, 1974) obsessed with the small details of dress (Wolfe, 1966), defined, like Tom Wolfe's pernickety New York lawyers in the angle of a shirt collar, measured as precisely as the vents in his custom-made jacket; by the shape of his hand-made shoes.

Unlike the defiantly obtrusive teddy boys, the mods were more subtle and subdued in appearance: they wore apparently conservative suits in respectable colours, they were fastidiously neat and tidy. Hair was generally short and clean, and the mods preferred to maintain the stylish contours of an impeccable 'French crew' with invisible lacquer rather than with the obvious grease favoured by the more overtly masculine rockers. The mods invented a style which enabled them to negotiate smoothly between school, work and leisure, and which concealed as much as it stated. Quietly disrupting the orderly sequence which leads from signifier to signified, the mods undermined the conventional meaning of 'collar, suit and tie', pushing neatness to the point of absurdity. And as Dave Laing remarks (1969) 'there was something in the way they moved which adults couldn't make out'; some intangible detail (a polished upper, the brand of a cigarette, the way a tie was knotted) which seemed strangely out of place in the office or class-room.

Somewhere on the way home from school or work, the mods went 'missing': they were absorbed into a 'noonday underground' (Wolfe, 1969) of cellar clubs, discotheques, boutiques and record shops which lay hidden beneath the 'straight world' against which it was ostensibly defined. An integral part of the 'secret identity' constructed here beyond the limited experiential scope of the bosses and teachers, was an emotional affinity with black people (both here and, via soul music, in the U.S.A.): an affinity which was transposed into style. The hard-core Soho mod of 1964, inscrutable behind his shades and 'stingy brim' only deigned to tap his feet (encased in 'basket weaves' or Raoul's originals) to the more esoteric soul imports (Tony Clarke's '(I'm the) Entertainer', James Brown's 'Papa's Got a Brand New Bag', Dobie Gray's '(I'm in with) The In Crowd' or Jamaican ska (Prince Buster's 'Madness'). More firmly embedded than either the teds or the rockers in a variety of jobs which made fairly stringent demands on their appearance, dress and 'general demeanour' as well as their time, the mods placed a correspondingly greater emphasis on the weekend. They lived in between the leaves of the commercial calendar, as it were (hence the Bank Holiday occasions, the weekend events, the 'all-niters'), in the pockets of free time which alone made work meaningful. During these leisure periods (painfully extended, in some cases, through amphetamine) there was real 'work' to be done: scooters to be polished, records to be bought, trousers to be pressed, tapered or fetched from the cleaners, hair to be washed and blow-dried (not just any old hair-drier would do, according to a mod interviewed by the *Sunday Times* in August 1964, it had to be 'one with a hood').

In the midst of all this frantic activity, the Black Man was a constant, serving symbolically as a dark passage down into an imagined 'underworld ... situated beneath the familiar surfaces of life' where another order was disclosed: a beautifully intricate system in which the values, norms and conventions of the 'straight' world were inverted.

Here, beneath the world's contempt, there were different priorities: work was insignificant, irrelevant; vanity and arrogance were permissible, even desirable qualities, and a more furtive and ambiguous sense of masculinity could be seen to operate. It was the Black Man who made all this possible: by a kind of sorcery, a sleight of hand, through 'soul', he had stepped outside the white man's comprehension. Even as the Entertainer he was still, like the mods, in service to the Man and yet he was a past master in the gentle arts of escape and subversion. He could bend the rules to suit his own purposes, he could elaborate his own private codes and skills and a language which was at once brilliant and opaque: a mask of words: 'a crest and a spurs'. He could inhabit a structure, even alter its shape without ever once owning it, and throughout the mid-60s he provided the hidden inspirational stimulus ('outta sight' in the words of James Brown) for the whole mod style.

18   CATCH A FIRE – TIMOTHY WHITE

Ska and bluebeat were as much a part of a Mod's musical diet as r'n'b and it was this that helped create the clubs in which all races mixed. Here's a little potted history of the music from a fine book on Bob Marley.

"As fond as Jamaicans were of American blues, they went wild when Fats Domino, Smiley Lewis, Huey Smith and the Clowns, Lloyd Price and other New Orleans artists took the sound a step further with a double shot of the Crescent City's unique rockin' rhythms. It was a strutting, half-stepping "second line" approach to R&B, the tempo incorporating the New Orleans-based dirges and jump-for-joy perambulations of jazz funerals; the Latin-tinged bass patterns of cathouse pianists like Jelly Roll Morton; rhumba, samba and the mambo of Perez Prado; the barrelhouse boogie-woogie of Kid Stormy Weather, Sullivan Rock, Robert Bertrand, Archibald, Champion Jack Dupree and Professor Longhair; and the chant-along exaltations of the traditional black Mardi Gras fraternal societies (known as 'Indian' tribes).

Jamaican bands began covering U.S. R&B hits, but the more adventurous took the nuts and bolts of the sound and melded them with energetic jazz conceits – particularly in the ever-present horn section – and emerged around 1956 with a hybrid concoction christened "ska." Ernest Ranglin, the stellar jazz-rooted Jamaican guitarist who backed up the Wailers on such ska classics as "Love and Affection" and "Cry to Me," says the word was coined by musicians "to talk about the skat! skat! skat! scratchin' guitar strum that goes behind."

Practically overnight, ska spawned a major Jamaican industry called the Sound System, whereby enterprising record shop disc jockeys with reliable American connections for 45s would load a pair of hefty PA speakers into a pickup truck and tour the island from hilltop to savanna, spinning the latest hits by the Fat Man and Joe Jones or tunes by local favorites like Kentrick "Lord Creator" Patrick and Stranger Cole. For added effect, the journeyman DJs gave themselves comic-book nom de plumes reminiscent of those of the early calypsonians: King Edwards, V-Rocket, Sir Coxsone Downbeat, Prince Buster. They would show up at the open-air dances dressed in gold lamé waistcoats, black leather Dracula capes, imitation ermine robes, Lone Ranger masks and rhinestone-studded crowns, waving a thumb-high stack of the island's most exclusive singles in one hand and an ornate pistol or night-searing machete in the other. The competition among DJs for the most current U.S. and Jamaican singles grew so heated that they covered the labels of the 45s with black paper or scratched them off altogether. Obviously it was a lot harder to keep up with rivals when you didn't know the name of the record or the artist causing the latest furore. Frustrated parties often settled their differences in a back alley or a lonely stretch of bush with pistols and ratchets (razor-sharp German switchblade knives).

The ska craze spread to London in the late 1950s and early 1960s, where an expanding West Indian population and curious Britons packed the "shebeens" (sleazy, unlicensed basement clubs) and Sound System dances to drink Long Life Lager, smoke ganja and revel in the tumult created by island recordings and visiting performers. In the United Kingdom, ska soon came to be called "bluebeat" in deference to Melodisc Records' BlueBeat label which started releasing tunes by such Jamaican groups as Laurel Aitken and the Carib Beats, Basil Gabbidon's Mellow Larks, and Desmond Dekker and the Aces. Encouraged by Jamaican audiences, English organist Georgie Fame added selections from the latest BlueBeat releases to his sets at London's Flamingo Club. Fame went on to record several ska-based singles on the R&B Disc label, the best being "Orange Street" and "JA Blues". At the same time, the Jamaican musicians in London picked up on the funky jazz of organist Jimmy Smith and saxman Lou Donaldson and took it back home with them.

But this music probably would have remained a mere curiosity were it not for the efforts of a white Anglo-Jamaican of aristocratic lineage named Chris Blackwell. As a hobbylike business venture, he had set up a small-scale distribution network for ethnic records. But he had a vision about the potential appeal of Jamaicans oscillating answer to the blues.

In 1962, Blackwell took his tiny Blue Mountain/Island label to England, purchased master tapes produced in Kingston and released them in Britain on Black Swan, Jump Up, Sue and the parent label, Island. Among his initial artists were Jimmy Cliff, Lord Creator, Wilfred "Jackie" Edwards, the Blues Busters, Derrick Morgan, trombonist Don Drummond and the Skatalites, and Bob Marley, whose first singles on Island were issued under the name Robert Marley. In England, Blackwell struck up a synergism with the fashion-conscious mod and skinhead teenage movements through his seminal Jamaican rock records. But the major breakthrough came when Millie Small, an adenoidal pixie he managed, scored a huge U.S. hit in 1964 with "My Boy Lollipop," which showcased the guitar of Skatalite Ernest Ranglin and an unsung harpist from Jimmy Powell and the Five Dimensions.

19 PARALLEL LIVES – PETER BURTON

The link between the gay scene and the Mod landscape is obvious but not well documented. Here Peter Burton nicely draws the parallels

The best discovery of all was the Lounge in Whitehall, a coffee-bar which lurked in the shadow of Scotland Yard. Run by an attractive and gay ex-policeman, the Lounge was the first venue in London for predominantly gay teenagers with an eye to style and an ear for music. Sadly, it didn't last long. Yet the Lounge deserves a niche in gay history simply because it was the forerunner of and the inspiration for one of the most fancily remembered clubs of that era: Le Duce.

By the mid Sixties, everything was changing. Those of us from the immediate post-war generation were developing our own tastes and inventing our own styles. We were evolving our own look and we had adopted our own music. We had found the drug we wanted to take and we had a language of our own – albeit a language that some gay men had been using for years.

Though those of us who used the Lounge and later Le Duce were gay, we shared many things in common with the other youth group who'd sprung up at about the same time: the Mods. In fact, the premiere Mod club – the Scene in Ham Yard behind Shaftesbury Avenue – was basically a straight version of Le Duce.

Economically, those who frequented the Scene and Le Duce both came from the same working-class – South and East London – backgrounds. Both groups paid the same attention to clothes – both groups looked much alike. Not surprising, really, as their clothes came from the same shops – initially Vince in Carnaby Street (whose catalogue of swim and underwear could *almost* be classified as an early gay magazine) and eventually from the John Stephen shops in the same street. Both groups took the same drug – basically 'speed', alternatively known as 'purple hearts', 'blues', 'doobs' or 'uppers.' Blues was the name we used most, with uppers the most common second choice.

Part of the ritual of the weekend was waiting for the blues to arrive or trekking off to someone's flat to collect them. Blues gave you energy, they kept you awake for the all-night sessions – if straight at the Scene; if gay at Le Duce. They gave you confidence. You felt you could talk to anyone; you could dance all night.

And dancing was important. As was the music that was popular with the Mods and the young gays who frequented Le Duce.

The two groups shared the same music. The mid-Sixties saw the slow beginnings of acceptance of black music – soul, blue beat, ska (which subsequently transmuted into reggae) and Tamla Motown. Except for isolated instances, none of these records were chart hits – certainly not on first release.

Records by performers like Prince Buster or Desmond Dekker and the Aces had to be searched for – and were most commonly found in specialist shops. They certainly weren't the kind of thing you'd hear on the radio – the BBC would have rather packed up shop than play the blatantly sexual, patently 'rude' songs by the likes of Prince Buster. Nor were the performers to be seen on the television music programmes of the day. It was all a bit too raw, and the media were really interested only in the clean-cut (the naughty but nice Beatles) or the acceptably watered down (the Rolling Stones).

Early Motown was 'gay music' every bit as much as Hi-Energy is now. Today, listening to songs like the Marvelettes' 'When You're Young and in Love', Martha Reeves and the Vandellas' 'Third Finger, Left Hand' (the wonderful 'B' side to 'Jimmy Mack'), Jimmy Ruffin's 'What Becomes of the Broken Hearted?' and 'I've Passed This Way Before', the Supremes' 'Stop in the Name of Love', Marvin Gaye's 'I Heard it Through the Grapevine', the Isley Brothers' 'This Old Heart of Mine (Been Broke a Thousand Times)', the Four Tops' 'Reach Out, I'll Be There' and 'Standing in the Shadows of Love', The Temptations' 'My Girl' and 'Ain't Too Proud to Beg', Mary

Wells' 'My Guy' or Smokey Robinson and the Miracles' 'You've Really Got a Hold on Me' and 'I Gotta Dance (To Keep From Crying)' – I realise how romantic and deeply sentimental they were. But they spoke directly to *us*.

This wasn't mass-produced music accepted by all and sundry. It seemed – to us – to be our exclusive preserve. Speeding out of our minds, generally filled with a sense of well-being and affection towards our fellows, we *were* sentimental and romantic. Whilst speed might have encouraged aggression in the Mods, it seemed to heighten our emotional feelings.

As we danced along to Motown's idealistic songs, we fell in love. We fell in love every weekend. Often affairs were brief – started on Sunday morning, over by Monday night. But the high obtained from the speed, the music and the companionship meant that these transitory flings were passionate and intense. And who is to say they were any less valid than romances which last for weeks, months, years?

We didn't listen to much 'white' music. Most of what was around seemed unutterably bland and wet. Almost the only white music we listened to was that performed by singers who had been influenced by black American soul music – who themselves had soul. The Righteous Brothers' 'You've Lost That Lovin' Feeling' – with a blockbuster Phil Spector production – hit the right emotional button. Dusty Springfield's 'You Don't Have to Say You Love Me' was another firm favourite. But then we all agreed – Dusty, with her panda eye makeup and stiffly lacquered beehive hairdo, was always guaranteed to crank out a good heart-rending number sung with as much soul as any white singer could decently manage.

20   THE LONELY LONDONERS – SAMUEL SELVON

When the Trinidadian writer Sam Selvon died, Martin Amis confessed he had never heard of him. Which says a lot about the gulf between talent and recognition. Sam Selvon came to Britain in the early '50s and wrote novels concerning the West Indian experience. This is by far his best effort and was published well before Absolute Beginners. *For me this section captures the magic of London and shows great attention to clothes and style.*

And once he had a date with a frauline, and he make a big point of saying he was meeting she by Charing Cross, because just to say 'Charing Cross' have a lot of romance in it, he remember it had a song called 'Roseann of Charing Cross.' So this is how he getting on to Moses:

'I meeting that piece of skin tonight, you know.' And then, as if it not very important, 'She waiting for me by Charing Cross Station.'

Jesus Christ, when he say 'Charing Cross,' when he realise that is he, Sir Galahad, who going there, near that place that everybody in the world know about (it even have the name in the dictionary) he feel like a new man. It didn't matter about the woman he going to meet, just to say he was going there made him feel big and important, and even if he was just going to coast a lime, to stand up and watch the white people, still, it would have been something.

The same way with the big clock they have in Piccadilly Tube Station, what does tell the time of places all over the world. The time when he had a date with Daisy he tell her to meet him there.

'How you don't know where it is?' he say when she tell him she don't know where it is. 'Is a place that everybody know, everybody does have dates there, is a meeting place.'

Many nights he went there before he get to know how to move around the city, and see them fellars and girls waiting, looking at they wristwatch, watching the people coming up the escalator from the tube. You could tell that they waiting for somebody, the way how they getting on. Leaning up there, reading the Evening beers, or smoking a cigarette, or walking round the circle looking at clothes in the glasscase, and every time people come up the escalator, they watching to see, and if the person not there, they relaxing to wait till the next tube come. All these people there, standing up waiting for somebody. And then you would see a sharp piece of skin come up the escalator, in a sharp coat, and she give the ticket collector she ticket and look around, and same time the fellar who waiting throw away his cigarette and you could see a happy look in his face, and the girl come and hold his arm and laugh, and he look at his wrist-watch. Then the two of them walk up the steps and gone to the Circus, gone somewhere, to the theatre, or the cinema, or just to walk around and watch the big life in the Circus.

Lord, that is life for you, that is it. To meet a craft there, and take she out some place.

'What you think, Moses?' he ask Moses.

'Ah, in you I see myself, how I was when I was new to London. All them places is like nothing to me now. Is like when you back home and you hear fellars talk about Times Square and Fifth Avenue, and Charing Cross and gay Paree. You say to yourself, "Lord, them places must be sharp." Then you get a chance and you see them for yourself, and is like nothing.'

'You remember that picture *Waterloo Bridge*, with Robert Taylor? I went down by the bridge the other night, and stand up and watch the river.'

'Take it easy,' Moses say wearily.

But Galahad feel like a king living in London. The first time he take a craft out, he dress up good, for one of the first things he do after he get a work was to stock up with clothes like stupidness, as if to make up for all the hard times when he didn't have nice things to wear.

So this is Galahad dressing up for the date: he clean his shoes until they shine, then he put on a little more Cherry Blossom and give them a extra shine, until he could see his face in the leather. Next he put on a new pair of socks – nylon splice in the heel and the toe. He have to put on woollen underwear, though is summer. Then the shirt – a white Van Heusen. Which tie to wear? Galahad have so much tie that whenever he open the cupboard is only tie he seeing in front of him, and many times he just put out his hand and make a grab, and whichever one come he wear. But for this date he choose one of those woollen ties that the bottom cut off. Before he put on trousers and jacket he comb his hair. That is a big operation for Galahad, because he grow the hair real long and bushy, and it like a clump of grass on the head. First, he wet the hair with some water, then he push his finger in the haircream jar and scoop out some. He rub the cream on his hands, then he rub his hands in his head. The only mirror in the room is a small one that Galahad have tie on to the electric light cord, and the way he have it, it just a little bit higher than he is, so while he combing the grass he have to sort of look up and not forward. So this comb start going through the grass, stumbling across some big knot in Galahad hair, and water flying from the head as the comb make a pass, and Galahad concentrating on the physiognomy, his forehead wrinkled and he turning the head this way and that. Then afterwards he taking the brush and touching the hair like a tonsorial specialist, here and there, and when he finish, the hair comb well.

When Galahad put on trousers the seam could cut you, and the jacket fitting square on the shoulders. One thing with Galahad since he hit London, no foolishness about clothes: even Moses surprise at the change. Now if you bounce up Galahad one morning by the tube station when he coming from work, you won't believe is the same fellar you did see coasting in the park the evening before. He have on a old cap that was brown one time, but black now with grease and fingerprint, and a jacket that can't see worse days, and a corduroy trousers that would shame them ragandbone man. The shoes have big hole, like they laughing, and so Galahad fly out the tube station, his eyes red and bleary, and his body tired and bent up like a piece of wire, and he only stop to get a *Daily Express* by the station. For Galahad, like Moses, pick up a night work, because it have more money in it. He wasn't doing electrician, but with overtime he grossing about ten so why worry? So while other people going to work, Galahad coming from work. He does cross the road and go by the bakery and buy a hot bread to take home and eat. This time so, as he walking, he only studying sleep, and if a friend bawl out 'Aye, Galahad' he pass him straight because his mind groggy and tired.

But when you dressing, you dressing. Galahad tailor is a fellar in the Charing Cross Road that Moses put him on to and the tailor surprise that Galahad know all the smartest and latest cut. He couldn't palm off no slack work on the old Galahad at all. And one thing, Galahad not stinting on money for clothes, because he get enough tone when he land up in tropical and watchekong. Don't matter if the test tell him twenty guineas or thirty-five pounds, Galahad know what he want, and he tell the fellar is all right, you go ahead, cut that jacket so and so, and don't forget I want a twenty-three bottom on the trousers.

And the crowning touch is a long silver chain hanging from the fob, and coming back into the side pocket.

So, cool as a lord, the old Galahad walking out to the road, with plastic raincoat hanging on the arm, and the eyes not missing one sharp craft that pass, bowing his head in a polite 'Good evening' and not giving a blast if they answer or not. This is London, this is life oh lord, to walk like a king with money in your pocket, not a worry in the world.

Is one of those summer evenings, when it look like night would never come, a magnificent evening, a powerful evening, rent finish paying, rations in the cupboard, twenty pounds in the bank, and a nice piece of skin waiting under the big clock in Piccadilly Tube Station. The sky blue, sun shining, the girls ain't have on no coats to hide the legs.

'Mummy, look at that black man!' A little child, holding on to the mother hand, look up at Sir Galahad!

'You mustn't say that, dear!' The mother chide the child.

But Galahad skin like rubber at this stage, he bend down and pat the child cheek, and the child cower and shrink and begin to cry.

'What a sweet child!' Galahad say, putting on the old English accent, 'What's your name?'

But the child mother uneasy as they stand up there on the pavement with so many white people around: if they was alone she might have talked a little, and asked Galahad what part of the world he come from, but instead she pull the child along and she look at Galahad and give him a sickly sort of smile, and the old Galahad, knowing how it is, smile back and walk on.

21 ABSOLUTE BEGINNERS – COLIN MACINNES

One of the best London novels ever, Absolute Beginners *unwittingly but brilliantly captures the Mod scene at its birth. It is easily MacInnes' best novel, written suitably enough above a tailors in London's West End.*

But this particular evening, I had to call at a teenage hut inside Soho, in order to contact two of my models, by names Dean Swift and the Misery Kid. Now, about Soho, there's this, that although so much crap's written about the area, of all London quarters, I think it's still one of the most authentic. I mean, Mayfair is just top spivs stepping into the slippers of the former gentry, and Belgravia, like I've said, is all flats in houses built as palaces and Chelsea – well! Just take a look yourself, next time you're there. But in Soho, all the things they say happen, do: I mean, the vice of every kink, and speakeasies and spielers and friends who carve each other up, and, on the other hand, dear old Italians and sweet old Viennese who've run their honest, unbent little businesses there since the days of George six, and five, and backward far beyond. And what's more, although the pavement's thick with tearaways, provided you don't meddle it's really a much safer area than the respectable suburban fringe. It's not in Soho a sex maniac leaps out of a hedge on to your back and violates you. It's in the dormitory sections.

The coffee spot where I hoped I'd find my two duets was of the kind that's now the chic-est thing to date among the juniors – namely, the pig-sty variety, and adolescent bum's delight. I don't exaggerate, as you'll see. What you do is, rent premises that are just as dear as any other, rip up the linos and tear out the nice fittings if there happen to be any, put in thick wood floors and tables, and take special care not to wipe the cups properly, or sweep the butts and crusts and spittle off the floor. Candles are a help or, at a pinch, non-pearl 40-watt blue bulbs. And a juke-box just for decoration, as it's considered rather naive to *use* one in these places.

This example was called Chez Nobody, and sure enough, sitting far apart from each other at distant tables, were the Dean and the Misery Kid. Though both are friends of mine, and, in a way, even friends of each other, these two don't mix in public, on account of the Dean being a sharp modern jazz creation, and the Kid just a skiffle survival, with horrible leanings to the trad. thing. That is to say, the Kid admires the groups that play what is supposed to be the authentic music of old New Orleans, i.e., combos of booking-office clerks and quantity-surveyors' assistants who've handed in their cards, and dedicated themselves to blowing what they believe to be the same note as the wonderful Creoles who invented the whole thing, when it all long ago began.

If you know the contemporary scene, you could tell them apart at once, just like you could a soldier or sailor, with their separate uniforms. Take first the Misery Kid and his trad. drag. Long, brushless hair, white stiff-starched collar (rather grubby), striped shirt, tie of all one colour (red today, but it could have been royal-blue or navy), short jacket but an old one (somebody's riding tweed, most likely), very, very, tight, tight, trousers with wide stripe, no sox, short *boots*. Now observe the Dean in the modernist number's version. College-boy smooth crop hair with burned-in parting, neat white Italian rounded-collared shirt, short Roman jacket *very* tailored (two little vents, three buttons), no-turn-up narrow trousers with 17-inch bottoms absolute maximum, pointed-toe shoes, and a white mac lying folded by his side, compared with Misery's sausage-rolled umbrella.

Compare them, and take your pick! I would add that their chicks, if present, would match them up with: trad. boy's girl – long hair, untidy with long fringes, maybe jeans and a big floppy sweater, maybe bright-coloured never-floralled, never-pretty dress … smudged-looking's the objective. Modern jazz boy's girl – short hemlines, seamless stockings, pointed-toed high-heeled stiletto shoes, crepe nylon rattling petticoat, short blazer jacket, hair done up into the elfin style. Face pale – corpse colour with a dash of mauve, plenty of mascara.[…]

If you have a friend who's a junkie, like I have the Dean, you soon discover there's no point whatever discussing his addiction. It's as senseless as discussing love, or religion, or things you only feel if you feel them, because the Dean, and I suppose all his fellow junkies, is convinced that this is "a mystic way of life" (the Dean's own words), and you and I, who don't jab hot needles in our arms, are just going through life missing absolutely everything worthwhile in it. The Dean always says, life's just kicks. Well, I agree with him, so it is, but personally, it seems to me the big kick you should try to get by how you live it sober. But tell that to the Dean!

Why I'd not recently seen him, is that he'd until then been away inside. This has fairly often happened to the Dean, owing to his breaking into chemists' shops, and as he suffers a lot when he's cut off from the world and all it gives in there, he doesn't like you to refer to it when he emerges. At the same time, he *does* like you to say you're glad to see him once again, so it's all a trifle dicey.

"Hail, squire," I said. "Long time no see. How is you are we? Won't you say tell?"

The Dean smiled in his world-weary way. "Doesn't this place stink?" he said to me.

"Well, certainly, Dean Swift, it does, but do you mean its air, or just its atmosphere?"

"The both. The only civilised thing about it," the Dean continued, "is that they let you *sit* here, when you're skint."

The Dean gazed round at the teenage products like a concentration camp exterminator. I should explain the Dean, though only just himself an ex-teenager, has sad valleys down his cheeks, and wears a pair of steel-rimmed glasses (which he takes off for our posing sessions), so that his Dean-look is habitually sour and solemn. (The Swift part of the thing comes from his rapid disappearance at the approach of any cowboys. You're talking to him and then, tick-tock! he's vanished.) I could see that now the Dean, as usual when skinned and vicious, was going to engage in his favourite theme, i.e. the horror of teenagers. "Look at the beardless microbes!" he exclaimed, loud enough for everyone to hear. "Look at the pram products at their plotting and their planning!"

And, as a matter of fact, you could see what he meant, because to see the kids hunched over the tables it *did* look as if some conspiracy was afoot to slay the elder brethren and majorities. And when I'd paid, and we went out in the roads, even here in this Soho, the headquarters of the adult mafia, you could everywhere see the signs of the un-silent teenage revolution. The disc shops with those lovely sleeves set in their windows, the most original thing to come out in our lifetime, and the kids inside them purchasing guitars, or spending fortunes on the songs of the Top Twenty. The shirt-stores and bra-stores with cine-star photos in the window, selling all the exclusive teenage drag I've been describing. The hair-style saloons where they inflict the blow-wave torture on the kids for hours on end. The cosmetic shops – to make girls of seventeen, fifteen, even thirteen, look like pale rinsed-out sophisticates. Scooters and bubble-cars driven madly down the roads by kids who, a few years ago, were pushing toy ones on the pavement. And everywhere you go the narrow coffee bars and darkened cellars with the kids packed tight, just whispering, like bees inside the hive waiting for a glorious queen bee to appear.

"See what I mean," the Dean said.

And the chicks, round the alleys, on that summer afternoon! Heavens, each year the teenage dream-girl has grown younger, and now, there they were, like children that've dressed up in their fashionable aunties' sharpest clothes – and suddenly you realise that it's not a game, and that these chicks mean business, and that it's not so much you, one of the boys, they aim their persons at, as their sheer, sweet, energetic legs walk down the pavement three by three, but no, at quite adult numbers, quite mature things, at whose eyes they shoot confident, proud looks there's no mistaking.

"Little madams," said the Dean.

"There you go!" I answered.

Here Dean Swift stopped us in his tracks.

"I tell you," he said, pulling his US-striped and rear-buckled cap down over his eyes, "I tell you something. These teenagers are ceasing to be rational, thinking, human beings, and turning into mindless butterflies. And they're turning into butterflies all of the same size and colour, that have to flutter round exactly the same flowers, on exactly the same gardens. Yes!" he exclaimed at a group of kiddos coming clicking, cracking prattling by. "You're nothing but a bunch of butterflies!"

But the kidettes took no notice of the Dean whatever, because just at that moment... there! In his hand-styled car with his initials in its number, there sped by the newest of the teenage singing raves, with beside him his brother, and his composer, and his chicklet, and his Personal Manager, so that all that was missing was his Mum. And the kids waved, and the young Pied Piper waved his free hand back, and everyone for a few seconds was latched on to the glory.

"Singer!" cried the Dean out after him. "Har, Har!"

22 LIMELIGHT BLUES – TONY PARSONS

One of the NME *writers who inspired me to write in the first place. Parsons left the* NME *to write a succession of novels. His obvious love for Modernism is displayed here with only one detail – the reference to Brighton beach battles – jarring the reader. Whatever you think about Parsons now the boy still loves a good suit.*

The minute *Ready Steady Go!* faded from the TV screen – Idiot's Lantern, Idiot's Lantern, David Lazar chanted to himself at slow moments in his parents' lounge and his place of work – he was heading for the bright lights of the real world.

He slammed the door – he liked to slam doors when he was speeding. Holloway was dim and drab even on a Friday night FRIDAY NIGHT! – and the house he was coming from looked no better than all the others. But it didn't matter anymore. He knew where the only place to be was. And he was heading there.

There was justice in the private world where he was heading, fast feet in shoes from Stan's of Battersea.

The creeps in the team at the agency thought they had the world on a leash and they would never be so wrong. They had the education, the aren't-you-a-lucky-boy grammar school education that his parents still hadn't forgiven him for throwing aside, they had the salary and the comfy nest in the Home Counties and the nice new classless (they hoped) accent and they had *nothing*.

SLOBS!

Vengeance was Mod.

He was fifteen and he was the best-dressed man in the whole big building. He spent more money on clothes in a week than they spent in a month – despite the disparity between their expense account padded salaries and the handful of peanuts in his wage packet. He had more full-blooded *pride* in himself than they would believe possible. Yet they were too smug and stupid to see the clues right under their snouts.

Mod was invisible to idiots.

They thought they were so special, the creeps on the team, but they reminded him of the commuters. The suits of the men in the Tube made him smile. What was the point in wearing a suit if you looked like a sack of potatoes in it? They stared at him, smiling at his dark rejection in the dark glass window as he sat speeding on the train, and they hated him, because he wore a suit beautifully and for pleasure, and they wore a suit as a convict wears a fetter. I commute to pleasure, he thought, and laughed. I think like an ad man already!

The commuters couldn't look at him and feel sorry for him and superior on their own behalf like they did with the deadheads, the Teds and Rockers. *Yobs.* He burned his speed stare into one inoffensive traveller's downcast eyes. *You* look like a yob to me, he concentrated, you look like a down-and-out in those clothes. Excuse me, but you're on the wrong train for Wapping Steps and that dear old cardboard box that you no doubt call home sweet home. This is the A Train.

He concentrated so hard that the commuter looked up from his paper. He took in the dark boy from head to toe and then began to read again, bringing the paper nearer his face. The dark boy looked like his surly blond son. They all had that look, the dark and the fair, the tall, the small, the sons of the soil and the daughters of immigrants. They were all related. They'd come from nowhere and you saw them everywhere. He'd see one tonight over the dinner table until he gave it some money so it could go out on the town. It was the look … the look of having been somewhere that made Planet Earth look like a one-horse town.

He didn't look at the boy again. They were harmless but they also seemed fearless. They liked to be looked at but not for too long.

But the Drynamil in the boy's brain had made him lose interest and he was staring now at the commuter directly opposite him. God, look at that suit. Put together in less time than it takes to get a buzz from a Black Bomber. David Lazar couldn't keep the good news to himself any longer. When the tube stopped at Oxford Circus he leaned across the aisle, tapped the man's *Daily News* and murmured: 'Bilgorri of Bishopsgate.'

'I beg your pardon?'

'My tailor.'

He was on the escalator into the night by the time the commuter realised he'd been insulted.

He walked speedwise down Great Windmill Street, both hands in his dark blue mohair pockets, his head down, his heart and soul and brain going up, up, up.

It was Friday night and he was a few steps away from The Scene.

David Lazar was a Mod.

David Lazar felt like God.

And that was putting it mildly.

Records played over monster fairground speakers in a little room with concrete walls – the best place in the world.

Sound came bouncing down, saturating the walls, the ceiling, the floor with the best black music that a white boy would ever hear. Later Ham Yard would be scattered with small groups of stunningly young people, talking and smoking and speeding, but right now they needed something bigger to wipe away the working week. David Lazar went through the door, wedged the brick back into place – the only ventilation The Scene Club needed, leaving you free to breathe that rarefied Mod air – and searched.

The boys stood all around, packed against concrete, dancing, drinking orange squash and stuff from unidentified hip flasks, but above all admiring each other.

Lazar moved through them – never pushing, pushing was lethal – smiling sometimes at people he had seen forever – life-long acquaintances – and keeping an eye on their clothes. Then he saw Kay Miller dancing in the corner, near the speakers, and he stopped still.

She had Cleopatra hair and very dark, very cool skin. She looked a lot like Juliette Greco but her brains were in her feet and *angst* was just another foreign word. She wore tight straight white hipsters and danced for an audience of one – a small blonde girl, identically dressed, who held two BEA air hostess bags. The girl was watching Kay's feet until she looked up and saw him.

He stood there staring, he stood through four records just

trying to get his courage up. He barely heard them – 'King of Kings', there was, followed by maybe 'Wipe Out' and then perhaps 'Hide And Go Seek – Part One'. When he heard the first notes of 'Ain't Love Good, Ain't Love Proud', he knew he could be there all night just growing older and getting nowhere.

He said, 'Hello, Kay.'

She didn't stop dancing. She looked at his feet and face and smiled. Then she closed her eyes. 'Hello, baby.'

He said, 'You dance better than Sandy Sarjeant.'

She nodded.

'You should be on *Ready Steady Go!*'

'I'm going to be, aren't I? Next week!'

He said, 'Can I dance with you?'

She frowned and shook her head. 'Waltz or tango?' She shook her head again. 'I mean, don't be stupid. Don't be kinky. Kay Miller means solo, everyone knows that.'

'Sorry.' He felt sick with embarrassment.

'That's okay.' she turned away slightly and he looked at her cool shoulder. Then she turned back and stopped dancing. 'Here, you look like one of these nervous kids whose quack fills them up with leapers once a month.'

'That's just what I am,' he said, and smiled, trying not to show her how hurt be was.

'Well, just lead the way, baby!' Kay Miller said. 'I was going to buy tonight – but if I have some of *yours*' – she made it sound as though she would be doing him a big, big favour by accepting his speed – 'I can get the shoes I want.'

She beckoned to the blonde girl, who struggled with her luggage and ran across the room behind them.

Outside they leaned against a wall. Kay swallowed Drynamil like gumdrops. Her friend wasn't much less reckless. The gumdrop substitutes made the friend quiet and solemn, but Kay made up for that. She talked non-stop. He loved it. Everyone knew Kay and Kay knew everything. She had been everywhere in the Mod world – The Goldhawk Club, Flamingo Club, Desiree Coffee Bar, Bank Holiday Brighton. Everywhere let her in free, because of the way she danced – only Brighton had told her never to come back again! She knew Phil the Greek who had once gone on *Ready Steady Go!* with a sawn-off shotgun.

'*Loaded!*'

'The Greek or the gun?'

She laughed, she liked that. 'Both!'

Jack; the best Jewish barber in London, was a vague relation.

She had once turned down Mickie Tenner because *Kay Miller means solo*. She had read a William Burroughs book ... she liked to read 'practical things, things about drugs'. Cathy MacGowan had once asked to borrow her comb and Kay Miller had said 'No.' Just that one word – 'No.' In front of everybody! She asked Lazar if he liked Dave Brubeck and when he admitted he'd never *heard* of him she said 'Oh, *well...*' and smiled, superior. She gave him a small card and told him to go to ATV House in the Strand next Friday to see her dance.

She looked at her silent friend. 'Paula, are you ok?' She peered closer and shook the little girl. 'You're a bit blue, aren't you, baby?'

'I'm having a come-down,' Paula said pessimistically.

'Paula, don't be kinky, baby! It's Friday night, not Saturday morning! You just need some more leapers.'

'I need more leapers,' repeated Paula, and looked at Oscar expectantly.

He had none left.

'Come on, don't be stingy,' said Kay.

'I'm going to make a connection. I'll be right back.'

'Get Durophet. Bombers!' shouted Kay happily.

He went back into the Scene and into the lavatory. He had to get pills, as many as it took to keep her high and happy and away from the crowds. He had money – he'd been going to buy an Arrow shirt Saturday morning. It didn't matter. Arrow shirts were made by the thousand. Kay Miller was an original.

In the lavatory were boys who had watched him go out into Ham Yard with Kay, boys who he knew she had been seen around with in the past. But not one of them stared or shoved or threatened him as he carried out the transaction. The Drynamil and Durophet had turned their libido down so low that dancing was the only physical activity solipsistic enough to tempt them. Kay was beautiful, a good girl, a prize, but they would rather look than touch. And she was known to feel just the same way – she thought like a Mod, not like a sort. And he, Lazar, was a Mod, and they recognized it. So though they watched him buying the bombers, and though they knew who he was trying to impress, it was all right.

He somehow knew that none of them would ever befriend him, but so what? Pills and music were a Mod's friends, the props he turned to and relied on. Friendship, mawkish, jealous friendship was for drunken Rockers and Teds, inferior beings who needed to merge to feel big. Mods were units of perfect private enterprise, that's why they were such an impressive and frightening sight whenever they assembled.

Lazar spent the night with Kay, in the Scene and in the yard, watching her dance and hearing her talk. They talked of clothes and records and speed and now – she was a hedonist with a heart of gold, he decided. At one point he put his arm around her as they drank weak orange squash.

She shot him a poison look, daggers in her gorgeous slate grey eyes. 'If I want mauling I'll go down the Tottenham Royal. This isn't a marriage bureau, you know.'

'I didn't ask you to *marry* me, you know.'

'Oh shut up, just shut up.' she sighed. 'I'm sorry, but I like to be alone. Really alone. In a big crowd, in front of a big audience, totally alone. I can't stand being touched when I'm speeding.' She held out her hand. 'I'd better have another.'

'These are Black Bombers, Kay. They make blues look like Junior Aspirin. Don't you think you've had enough?'

Paula gasped at his impertinence.

Kay drew herself up to her full five-foot-five. 'I've had enough of *you*. Who do you think *you* are, some North London nobody to tell *Kay Miller* about pills? And one for Paula, please. Thank you.'

'The papers say they cause brain damage,' remarked Paula washing the pill down with orange squash.

'Yeah, they should know.'

At six a.m. the Scene closed. They were all out in the dawn grey streets. The Mods dissolved and made for their favourite coffee bars. At the Desiree they drank French coffee. Kay's white hipsters were immaculate but her face was crumpled and creased.

'I never wear make-up at weekends. See? I've known girls who do. God, they look awful. The way I see it … the way I see it is … if you're a Mod you just want to have a good time and keep clean. All a Mod is … all a Mod is is having self-respect … It's the most fabulous way of life you can ever imagine, that's all.' She slumped on to Paula's lap and closed her eyes. 'God, I feel awful.' Within two minutes she was asleep.

He was amazed. He thought she'd stay with him all weekend, that they'd roam the streets, *own* the streets, watch the clothes go by and at the end of the day make the Scene. To go through the door, with *her*!

'Is Kay ok?'

Paula looked gloomy. 'This is always the way. You'd better go home.'

He wandered into the Soho dawn, pale and squinting. A gaggle of teenaged girls swaggered up to him, holding on to each other for support. They were singing.

Don't take those purple pills, my love,
In the end they'll make you blue.
If you take those purple pills, my love,
Black death will follow you.

Then they laughed.

His money was gone. Kay was out for the count. He had to get the Tube home. He slumped in his seat. People looked at him as though he was a down-and-out. But it didn't matter. He was only living the most fabulous way of life you could imagine, that's all.

23 HEAVEN'S PROMISE – PAOLO HEWITT

Vibing off the aforementioned Sam Selvon, another writer to fire me up, I wanted to capture the Mod ethic of coming to London and devising your own moves until it creates the perfect lifestyle.

Walking down the long snaking tunnel to the grey dirty platforms, I passed numerous people out and about on their business and somehow the scene livelied me up somewhat, especially as the busker on the morning shift was a young dude coming on strong with a nice selection of Bob Marley tunes. I went to give him a coin as I do anyone who is not playing the obvious songs for my rule on buskers is a fair one. Nothing at all against The Beatles or Bob Dylan or Simon and Garfunkel, because they've all done their bit, but if I hear one more crooner singing "Yesterday" or "Knocking on Heaven's Door" then I will have no option but to immediately report them to the nearest authorities for gross public misconduct, and that especially applies to "Theme From The Deer Hunter."

This morning's musical selection featured Marley's "One Love/People Get Ready," and was sung with such conviction that you couldn't help but be moved by both singer and song.

Yet despite my good mood I soon found it to be temporary. Boarding the train to take me Westward Ho, the Sandra business reared up in my HQ and immediately took me right down. What hit me first, as I struggled to make sense of this morning's unexpected and unbelievable events, was that, without a doubt, all future missions, such as a stay in New York to crib off those DJ masters, were going to have to be put on ice until this crisis was sorted, one way or another.

That was for sure but there was something else starting to bug me out and that was a growing feeling that suddenly, I had no control whatsoever over my life. It was as if, like a terrible dream you have to wake yourself up from, I had become a lead character in a film I had no desire to be in and the director hadn't even told me the plot and dialogue and I was left to improvise like John Coltrane to make sense of it all.

Perhaps, I mused, that was precisely what life was, a huge mega budget epic with God directing us all purely for His own amusement, the biggest joke being that all us poor souls have been led to believe that we are somehow in charge of how the film starts and finishes.

No doubt about it, as the great Sam Cooke knew, a change was going to come and I would have to bend with it or lose badly and that was the truth, Ruth.

Only I didn't want to make that move and not when my runnings had finally started to come together. I had living quarters, cashola, a job which I could use as a springboard to the next level if I was sharp enough, but above all I had a certain kind of freedom which allowed me space in my life, a space that far too many are forced to give up the day they walk out of school and start taking orders from the bosses.

From an early age I had determined that I wanted no part of that nine to five scam and so, on the day I dumped my blazer where it belonged, I had put my all into becoming a DJ, dedicating all my spare hours to acquiring equipment and learning how best to use it, sharpening my skills so that I was not answerable to some greyer of a boss who would take delight in making your life a misery because his was so utterly sad.

To achieve that end I devised a routine that involves constantly tuning into the pirate radio stations scattered all over town, cluing up on various magazines for tip offs, visiting record shops at least three times a week, (except on Sundays when I head for record fairs or car boot sales) and forever using my HQ to put together various mixes in my head which I then try out at my yard where no one is looking.

Consequently, I am on first name terms with a lot of shop owners and fellow DJ's and many hours are spent talking over music, artists, name producers, record labels, new releases, old tunes discovered, clubs, musicians and anything else connected to this vast and rich world that I so delight in being a part of.

If others can't check for these lengthy conversations then they are deemed irrelevants although it must be stated that, on the whole, women are the exception to the rule. Gals like music a lot but the majority of them use it differently, and without the obsession.

It is of little interest or juice to them how a record came to be. If, for example, you tell them how Berry Gordy didn't want to release "What's Going On" by Marvin Gaye, or that Sly Stone covered "Que Sera Sera" because the papers thought he was loving Doris Day up, their eyes tend to glaze over and their minds wander of as if they had somewhere better to be.

Gals never check for such details but they certainly move in other mysterious ways which is why I was now bound Westward Ho, to seek urgent advice on the latest development in Sandra's life.

To be sure, I much prefer tube travel to any other and the reasons for my preference are many. It is easily the quickest way, barring delays and the like, to scoot around town, allowing you to travel to all points with relatively ease.

On the tube you have time to get up to all kinds of things that you put off at home, such as reading or thinking or even listening to tunes on your walkman, and before you know it, there, you've arrived at your destination.

I know that most prefer cars but I have seen too many of my links go from happy to mad within five minutes of driving in this city, with its crumbling roads, huge traffic jams and Mad Max drivers, that I wish to steer clear of such distress.

Of course, the tube is not perfect by any stretch of the HQ and it's even worse come the rush hour p.m. and the people cram in, just as they had to that morning, their exhausted pissed off faces as eloquent a testimony to the cruel nature of work as anything else.

Yet come the weekend it's slightly different because then most of them are travelling for pleasure and so I wasn't too surprised, as I pulled out Sam Selvon's *The Lonely Londoners*, to hear a loud West Country accent assail me with an, "Easy Mr. DJ man, how's your percentage of life?" and realised that it was none other than Sammy The Foot who was addressing me.

This is a character who I am on speaking terms with, such as I am with The Sherrif, Stinga or Jasmine, through my position at The Unity Club, and whose yard is in close proximity to mine.

Sammy The Foot frequents The Unity but the location of most of our meetings has been at clubs where jazz is the only music played and which always attracts a small but dedicated crowd who are normally some of the best movers in town.

Sammy The Foot is no exception, a jazz dancer of real

excellence, capable of busting the kind of athletic and gracious moves that make you ashamed to be within ten yards of him on the dancefloor as he goes into his routine.

When Sammy The Foot and his comrades, some of whom come from as far as Manchester to indulge in their passion, take to the floor, you know it is time to discreetly retire because that space is his true home and although he and his friends never flash it in a look-at-me-I'm-so-great manner, it is still best to simply pull back and watch, rather than compete in any way.

Furthermore, such is Sammy's love of jazz and dance, that his gears are all old style such as you see in fading pictures of various jazz musicians and their audience, his public attire often consisting of such items as large caps, zoot suits and brown and white spats, all of which give you the impression that Sammy just left The Cotton Club in Harlem and waltzed into the present. Today was no exception with Sammy sporting an eye-catching grey pin striped baggy suit, a small flower in the left lapel of his double breasted jacket, white shirt and flowered tie, a walking stick and two tone shoes. On his head, tipped at an angle, was a large trilby. Sammy looked every bit the celebrity that he aspired to be and this desire, so legend had it, was first nurtured in him many years ago when he made his first TV appearance, albeit unwittingly, as a little kiddiwink.

The story has it that Sammy was but seven years old when a general election was called and the local Conservative MP returned to Sammy's home base of Yeovil for the first time in years, a camera crew in tow with which to capture him on the campaign trail routine of kissing bambinos, cuddling old folk and blaming everyone but himself and his party for society's ills. Sammy's folks are Nigerians and you don't get too many of them to the pound in the British countryside. In fact, you don't get any so when the aspiring MP spotted Sammy and his mum out and about, innocently walking the High Street to get the shopping, he saw a unique chance to do something for race relations in this country.

"Hello, young man," the MP boomed picking up Sammy much to his astonishment, "what part of the world were you born in?" The camera zoomed in expectantly on a bewildered Sammy and the old smiling politico who, no doubt, was expecting the name of some far off exotic country that the British had "civilized" not so long ago to drop from Sammy's lips.

"Yeovil," Sammy said. "I come from Yeovil."

The MP, momentarily stunned and bewildered, froze and then quickly put down Sammy saying, with a smile as transparent as water, "Yes, of course you are. Now who's this pretty little girl over here?" and marched off, praying no one noticed his burning cheeks of embarrassment.

The whole sorry incident was briefly shown on TV that night but with the commentator's voice running over the film so all you saw was the MP cuddling Sammy and you never heard his words. Through it, Sammy became something of a cause célèbre in his hometown, with all the kids at his school treating him as a major figure, "because he was on telly", until three weeks later the MP was returned to Parliament with an increased majority and everyone forgot the incident and got on with their lives. No doubt the bug of holding centre stage had been planted in the young one from that point on, because whenever you saw him you couldn't help but be overwhelmed by his ability to walk in to any public place and have everything revolve around him and not vice versa, which is how it runs for the majority.

"Easy Sammy," I said, putting away my book, "how goes it?"

"Not too well Mr. DJ man", he replied sitting down next to me and smiling ever so graciously at the lady opposite who was obviously taken with his attire and demeanour.

"The Loved One is on my case again."

"Trouble with your gal?"

"She tells me that I pay more attention to dancing than I do her and soon she will walk if I do not change my ways." He shrugged his shoulders.

"But she'll come round. I knows it."

What's fascinating about Sammy is that the man's true vocation is not really dancing, although God knows he is a right little Nureyev when he gets going, but it is the art of acting that he has truly mastered. This is his main strength and the reason for my take on him came one night when, in an unguarded moment, he led me through the rhyme and reasons of his life. When Sammy quit Yeovil in his teens, the only offer of a job being at the helicopter factory, he arrived in the Capital knowing neither friend or foe, a major problem for a lot of faces who descend from the hinterlands looking to escape the dull local action of pubs, fights, marriage, mortgage, kids and death. In Sammy The Foot's case, the idea of hosting a TV show had grabbed him the strongest, a wish no doubt stemming from the infamous MP incident and with that view in mind, Sammy quit home and made for the Capital.

Shocked and troubled at first by the impersonal nature of this city, Sammy spent his first few months in a miserable bedsit, signing on and aimlessly wandering around town looking for a friendly face, going to bed at night not a little scared, until one day it dawned on him that if London was not to come to Sammy, why then, he must go to London and grab it by the scruff of the neck. Jazz music being his first love, a condition brought about by his mother's preoccupation with be-bop, Sammy sought out the underground jazz clubs and spent hours leaning against a wall, memorising the moves he witnessed on the dancefloor. Night-time, at home, he would, much to the annoyance of the neighbour below him, practise these moves for hours on end whilst during the day he scoured the Oxfam shops for suitable gears, knowing full well that when he made his entrance into the life, his eccentric gears style would instantly set him apart. He would also, he recognised, have to hide that part of his nature which was shy and retiring so that he would always exude poise and confidence, qualities that everyone is instantly attracted to if only because they wish some of it to rub off on themselves. Come the day that Sammy The Foot took to the dancefloor, it was with such style and grace that within weeks people were checking for this strangely dressed but brilliant mover and gravitating towards him. Sammy The Foot played his part, coming on mysterious, whetting people's appetites and all the time building up contacts. In no time at all, he had secured a relationship with a well off gal from the Surrey countryside and moved in with her but his constant drive towards fame meant that he spent a lot of time "at work," as he called his lengthy stay in club after club, and that had started to bug out his lady.

"She thinks I should be at home with her every night," he explained to me as we hurtled down the dark tunnel, the tube rocking from side to side, "but how am I to meet people if I don't make the rounds. You tell me."

I had no answer to his question and even if I had I wouldn't have spilt it because ten times out of ten it is never wise to get involved in a couple's runnings for the partner in distress only wants to hear what they want to hear, and no matter what you say or reason, their heart, not their head will guide them each and every time. As the heart has no use for reason, the only time to give forth your opinion is if your closest link comes to you for advice or wisdom and you state all of the above. Otherwise it is best to take the fifth on the grounds that you may incriminate yourself and a friendship, and as nothing is worth that, I changed the talk.

"You out and about last night, Sammy?"

"That is exactly my point," he said, determined to take the

weight off his shoulders by talking it through.

"Last night, there was an all nighter going off down Hammersmith way. I inform my lady that I will be present and correct and that I would very much like her to accompany me. She tells me, that she is sick of my stepping out, that I am just using her for cashola purposes and that if I do not stay in and miss the jam then we are finished. I tell her sure, babe. If that's what you want. But first I must go out and buy some cigarettes. Of course, once I am in the night air the bug bites me, so I figure I'll just slip over to the dance, spend half an hour at best and then return home.

"I reach the club and before I know it I am being approached by two TV people who are wishing to make a film about the jazz scene. We exchange numbers and I am to go and see them next week."

"That's great Sammy."

"Not for my lady it isn't. When I got home I tell her of my great fortune and that everything will be alright. She told me, "really". Then went back to sleep."

"So where are you heading for now."

"Blackpool."

"Blackpool?"

"Yes indeed. I am off to munch on rock and see the famous lights."

"And," I said cottoning on, "to attend the Jazz weekender that is going off there."

"Yes but look, if you see my gal you haven't seen me, okay? I am considering going invisible over the next few days just to get my head into shape over this sorry state of affairs."

"Sammy, none of my business but you have been with your gal longtime and you shouldn't distress her too much. At least bell her."

"Maybe," he said with a shrug and tossing a sly wink at the woman opposite who, having followed our every word with great indiscretion, promptly turned red and looked away, "and maybe not. I know what you're saying but she has to learn that I don't rush around for just my benefit but hers as well. If she can't see that, why then, what can she see?"

The train pulled into Kings Cross and Sammy jumped up. "Gotta slide, this is my stop. Go well, Mr. DJ man and no whispering in the corridors. I'll check you at The Unity soon. Know what I mean and mean what I know? Laters."

"Laters, Sammy."

24 TOBACCO ROAD – ALAN FLETCHER

Alan Fletcher is an original Mod from Nottingham who penned the novel to Quadrophenia *and has self published three fictional books. This is an extract from his third novel,* The Blue Millionaire *(available from Chainline Books, 149 Hilton Road, Mapperley, Nottingham) and brings the scooter into play.*

'I can't afford it.' Jed said

'Neither can I.' Dazz confided, briefly studying the look of disappointment which registered on his friend's face. The man in the showroom hovered at what in salesman's terms, was a polite distance. The two shot almost plaintive looks in his direction and then returned their gaze to the objects of their desire. Dazz's eyes were locked onto a Lambretta TV175 motor scooter. Jed's were focused on a Vespa GS150. The Lambretta was finished in white while the GS was painted in its original silver livery.

Jed put his right hand on the Vespa's handlebars and tamed the throttle. The rubber grip filed his fist, it felt good. It fitted. Perfectly. Without looking at his friend he spoke quietly, tentatively. 'We could go halves…'

'You buy the bike, I'll buy the bits.' Dazz answered immediately.

They were on the same wave length, tuned in exactly to each other's thoughts and powerless to break faith with the carefully declared and designed Mod protocols of trend and style.

A scooter without the designated accessory kit was nothing.

'They're both taxed 'til August '65' shouted the salesman who had now moved a couple of paces closer to them.

'Which one?' Jed turned to Dazz.

'The Lambretta!' Dazz said, climbing onto the TV's seat. Jed smiled and shook his head, 'The Vespa.'

Dazz turned side-saddle on the Lambretta's seat and ferreted in the pocket of his hipsters. The tight cut of the flat fronted trousers and the angle at which he was sitting on the bike made access to the single pocket difficult: but he was loathe to remove himself from the bike's seat for fear of surrendering the high ground in promoting his preference for the Lambretta.

'Toss you.' Dazz said, idly flicking a coin in the air.

'O.K.' Jed responded, keeping hold of the Vespa's twist grip. Both were of the opinion that possession was nine points of the law. Dazz caught the coin and set it up on the thumb and first finger of his right hand: along with the salesman they both watched the coin soar high towards the roof lights of the showroom.

'Heads!' called Jed as the florin reached the apex of its flight. Dazz caught it and turned it over onto his left wrist, keeping his right hand firmly over the coin. They looked at each other intensely. Their silence was punctuated by a shout from the salesman who was drawing closer by the minute.

'They've both got a full tank...'

They ignored him, looking first at each other then at Dazz's right hand as he slowly raised his palm to reveal the silver coin. The smile on Jed's face confirmed their joint purchase of a Vespa GS150 Motor Scooter as they both gazed on the Queen's head on the upside of the tossed coin. Dazz slipped off the Lambretta's seat and if looks could kill...

'The colour's crap!'

'We can change it!'

'Needs a new exhaust!'

'So! – we'll get one with a chrome tail pipe.'

'Just look at the fucking windscreen!' Dazz banged the full-sized windshield with disgust. The scratched perspex displaying the bike's £110 price tag quivered in fright.

'It'll look brilliant with a new fly-screen.' Jed remained resolute in his preference.

Dazz bent over the Vespa's seat and turned on the petrol at the tap. He floored the kick-start and the engine fired immediately. He revved the bike viciously and then let it idle, walking around to the rear of the bike.

''s a bit smoky...'

'Mixture screw needs a tweak, that's all –' Jed added, 'Started first time.'

Dazz smiled, conceding his friend's fair won choice and then killed the engine with the button on the handlebars. The engine died instantly, crisply. There was no pre-ignition. He credited this piece of mechanical data. The bike was sound. That had never been in dispute; but his naturally competitive nature had compelled him to try to change Jed's mind. It was just that he preferred the Lambretta – but he'd soon get over that.

The salesman was now breathing down their necks. Smell the sale – he could taste it.

Dazz knocked him down a tenner – that would buy them half a dozen mirrors at least. With the bargain finally struck the pair shook hands to cement their joint purchase and quickly worked out the broad parameters of the bike's shared usage. They'd make the arrangement work – and work in style.

While the clerk in the office was drawing up the purchase documents and sorting out the log book the salesman was salivating on his commission from the sale and they were already dreaming how on it, they would travel a million miles and break a million hearts.

'Have you got a spanner handy?' Dazz asked the salesman when he brought the bike's documents to them.

'Spanner?' the man looked puzzled, 'There's nothing wrong with it…'

'You don't think we're gonna ride it away with this geriatric crap on it do you?' Again Dazz rapped the windshield, bolt upright on the Vespa's handlebars. He smiled at the man's benign and blissful ignorance of the clearly defined nuance and detail of Mod.

'We're gonna ride it away?' Jed asked Dazz as the man went to the workshops for the spanner.

''Course we are!' Dazz replied, ''s ours now – right!'

'We haven't got any insurance yet.'

'Stuff the insurance! – we can sort that out tomorrow. You wanna ride it or what?'

'We've only got provisionals…'

Dazz smiled and shook his head. He pulled out a folded piece of paper from his back pocket. He waved it in front of Jed. 'Full licence – cars and motor cycles over 200cc.'

Jed frowned.

'It's my cousin's – same initials as me – I've borrowed it – indefinitely. He's in the Merchant Navy for the next couple of years at least.' Dazz smiled broadly. Jed's due respect for the legal requirements and obligations necessary to own and operate a motor scooter started to melt away as they both freed the bolts securing the windshield. The bike took on a different countenance as he loosened the fitting and helped his friend lift the attachment clear of the speedo cowl. By the time they were riding through the showroom doors all Jed's sense of responsibility had vanished completely. Mambo Italiano!

They flashed around the town, Dazz threading the Vespa through the traffic without mishap – more through luck than by accomplishment in his riding. Jed winced at some of Dazz's initial gear changes and late, violent braking, he was winded at least a couple of times as inertia slammed his chest into Dazz's back as the bike lurched to a standstill at some of the red lights they encountered around the town – but by the time they had taken in a couple of circuits of Broadmarsh and burned up and down the long drag of Arkwright Street Dazz had mastered the foibles of the bike's mechanical and handling characteristics and they both felt relaxed and easy with it. At one with the bike and the modern world. They clicked. They slotted in.

In pursuit of the true Mod style of riding the bike Dazz sat at the front edge of the seat and tucked himself in closely behind the front leg shields, his knees touching the gentle curves of Piaggio's carefully sculpted panel lines. The side of his shoes rested against the point where the running boards met the front panels' upward sweep. His toes hung out to the side of the bike. The geometrical relationship twixt tip of shoe and running board was of particular significance (it followed the lines laid down before). The shoe could be positioned at whatever angle you wished, providing it was *exactly* 45° to the horizontal! Jed knew that to conform with the decreed way of riding pillion he should be leaning well back over the rear wheel of the scooter, arms folded or behind his head; the snag was that the bike didn't have a back rest – yet. In a flagrant contravention of all the interests of safety he refused point blank to put his arms around Dazz's waist – so he gripped the bottom of the seat and was thus whisked white knuckled, around Nottingham.

Around The Broadmarsh they skirted and through the Lace Market they felt soulful – an Anglicised version of America's Sam and Dave on an Italian scooter (with their best threads soon to be protected by US Army Surplus). Method actors off Broadway. Eventually they entered Stanford Street: halfway up the road Dazz slowed the Vespa and turned it in a circle outside a doorway framed by two classical stone columns – the entrance to The Dungeon club.

The weekend for the Mods (local and itinerant) started there.

Dazz stopped outside the club, put his feet down to the floor and steadied the bike. Jed remained on the pillion seat. With neutral selected Dazz left the engine running and turned back to Jed.

'This is where we'll park it...' Dazz said, 'right outside the front door. Prime spot – right where everybody'll see it.'

Jed tapped him on the shoulder and shook his head. 'Over the road!' He pointed, smiling, 'It'll stand out more there!!'

Even before it was painted they could picture the bike on show in the outdoor gallery.

With their confidence on the GS now at high point Dazz rode the bike onto Maid Marian Way and negotiated the roundabout at the top, taking them down Friar Lane.

It was time to do a lap of honour around the Market Square. Slab Square. The focal point of the inner city. Meeting place and catwalk for the Nottingham Mods.

They turned left and skirted the northern edge of this stone acre past Griffin & Spalding. They waved to some of their acquaintances standing beneath the columns of the department store and turned in front of the Council House. Half a dozen scooters were parked on the concourse in front of the steps which led up to the entrance arches forming a verandah to the building. A crowd of the local Mods, boys and girls, were sitting on the bikes or milling around them. Some of the group turned to the crisp sound of the GS as Dazz eased off the throttle and coasted past them. They exchanged salutations with the Mods but Dazz didn't stop. Their bike glided past the Lambrettas and Vespas parked to their left. The glitter of freshly waxed cellulose and the shiny chromium and quicksilver of a hundred mirrors was bounced across to them by the afternoon sunlight. Soon their bike would take its place among the vanguard of the Nottingham Mods' fleet.

Soon, but not yet.

They had missed being part of the Easter showcase for the chrome of their generation, but had, during that weekend, taken time to suss out the mettle of the scooters which had flooded into the towns on the East Coast from three points of the compass. With their bike decked out they would be cast in a starring role at the August Bank Holiday rendezvous, if not the coastal excursions at Whitsun. No doubt about it.

As they left the Square along South Parade they were already on their way to transforming and customising the Vespa into an acceptable aspect of Mod.

Both side panels were dropped off at an electro-platers in a Bulwell back street: for three shillings and sixpence a square inch the pallid silver cowlings would be transformed into a pair of chrome breasts. Money hard earned would be money well spent.

Their next port of call was a boat builder in Norton Street, Radford. A set of transfer letters (a **G** and an **S**) seven inches high, black, edged in white, bought there would soon embellish the front panels. After the bike's colour was altered – radically. A smaller set of letters would soon spell the word **NOTTS** in a crescent sweep around the edge of the small fly screen when fitted. The transaction at the boat builders was completed by the purchase of another two letters – **D** & **J**. Their initials. These would be fixed along the bottom edge of the flyscreen. They had yet to work out the way they would be attached. Dazz was pitching for **DJ** as it was musical – DeeJay – (studiously ignoring the fact that his initial featured first!) Jed liked the sound of JD – it reminded him of a cool character in "The Dakotas" – an obscure American TV series – a Western which had a brief run late on Saturday nights in the early 60s.

So – compere or cowboy? The choice for the time being remained open to negotiation.

25 WEEKEND – IAN HEBDITCH

Ian is an original Mod, hailing from Portsmouth. This extract was written in 1969 as part of his University thesis entitled I Do Like To Be Beside The Seaside. *He is anxious to state that he would do a far better job now. Which may be true but I like the energy of this piece plus you get details of The Action live.*

I have attempted here to describe what life was like for a mod by relating the description of a typical weekend of the period in the language and style I think I would have used at the time.

Saturday morning, wake up, mum brings me breakfast then I get up and dress, casual because I'm going into town. Red check shirt, blue suede levi jacket and white jeans, comb my hair then off out, it's about ten thirty. I get my scooter out, a white Vespa G.S. with chrome bubbles and white-wall tyres, nothing else that would be too flash, and head off down to Southsea. I worked at a filling station evenings in the week so I've got a bit of cash.

I go first to the Guildhall Square, a coffee bar called Verrechia's to see some mates, Harry and Splif to get fixed for pills for the evening. Having completed my "shopping", down to the front, where the rest are. It's thick with scooters, blokes and girls are lounging about not doing a lot, so we go for a ride round. Back at the Guildhall there is a bit of a scrap going on with Old Bill, he tried to move a crowd of the mods on and one of them knocked his helmet off. We run the scooters onto the pavement for effect, but it looks as though it's all over, I notice they're putting Jimmer Smith into a Black Maria, poor old Jimmer, he's a mate of mine and I know his mum will kill him.

Anyway, it's time for a coke down the Manhattan, another coffee bar (this was the place where we would all congregate in the afternoons).

"Action's on tonight down the 'Cage'."

"Nice one."

"Got any doubs (pills)?"

"Too true."

"Spare?"

"Dunno see tonight. Who's that salt over there then."

Harry pipes up, "That's Gammy Gilbert's sister."

Universal gestures of disgust.

The juke box blares out Otis Redding records, and the conversation continues in this vein until about five when we start to filter off. I ride off home for my tea.

Dad's in a black mood, so I keep quiet, eat my tea at record pace and then run off upstairs for a bath, have a good soak. I'll be sweating a bit tonight I reckon.

After putting my copper coloured mohair suit on, tie and handkerchief, I go round to get my mate Jack, he's just got a new leather, two tone green, nice. Anyway, we head off down to Eastney where the Birdcage is.

It's about eight o'clock and there's already a big queue because the Action are a pretty popular band. I see Harry and get my tabs from him – thirty "French" Blues at sixpence a time. Rikki pulls up in his yellow Jaguar, "Hi lads" he says and we follow him straight in – a bit of luck that we didn't have to pay.

The Birdcage is very sumptuously finished with deep red carpets and drapes. We walk upstairs to the club itself. There's a fairly large dancing area with seating and tables on raised platforms at the sides, a smaller room at one end contains the bar. We buy cokes and wash down ten blues a piece with them, it was always amusing to see the boys trouping off down to the toilets with their cokes to chew their pills. We take them early because they take half an hour to take effect.

When we come back the place is beginning to get packed. Pete (the D.J.) is playing "You Don't Know Like I Know" by Sam and Dave, and "Mr. Jones", a sort of idiot bloke who wears straight clothes, is out dancing on his own and talking to a coke bottle like a lunatic, he doesn't need pills he's like it anyway. "Mr. Jones" was a sort of mascot at the Birdcage – he used to go every night and Rikki lets him in for free. He's part of the furniture and no-one takes much notice of him.

The atmosphere's getting pretty wild now and a lot of people are dancing, sometimes six or seven blokes in a ring, all pilled out of their tiny minds. Jack and me are starting to feel a bit blocked as well so, out with the chewing gum and onto the floor. Pete sees me and puts on the Impressions' "You've Been Cheating." He knows it's my favourite, so out we go, motion to a deuce (a pair of girls) and we're off. Jack's a really good dancer, slick and snappy, and I'm alright so the girls are well pleased for a dance. We have a couple, feeling really good then we see the band come out to tune up so we rush to the front. The place is so packed that there's not much room to dance anyway.

All round the stage there's a great crowd shouting for Reggie King, the leader. Instead we get Rikki, who cracks a few corny jokes, everyone boos and whistles madly until he introduces the Action. There's a massive cheer and Reggie King runs on stage. He's got a sweater with a target on it, smart I think. Finger thrust into his right ear (so he can hear if he's in tune over the sound of the band) he breaks into "Heatwave", it's deafening but the beat is really infectious, the Rickenbackers jangle with a peculiar note of their own and what with the pills and the band we feel tremendously elated. Everyone's cheering madly and clamouring to get nearer to the stage, Reggie's putting on a really wild show, getting down on his knees and really feeling what he's singing, we're right with him because we know most of the songs practically by heart. The first set ends after about an hour and we go for a coke and a breather.

Here is a good point to briefly describe the decoration round the stage. It consists of massive pop art placards, chevrons in black and white and targets, slogans are inscribed on them, "in crowd" and "Blast London" are typical examples, the last one refers to the strange inferiority complex we had as regards London. London got all the attention and publicity but we reckoned we were just as good, the Mods from London were admired and yet feared. Any visitor from London to the Birdcage earned instant respect. There was a big hole in the ceiling over the stage where Pete Townshend stuck his guitar through it, it was never repaired because it was a kind of status symbol for the club, "Ah, Townshend did that, what a night".

I look round there's a bit of action its the corner Fred Loverage and somehow his crew have caught a Southampton bloke and are pouring coke over his leather coat. I feel a bit sorry for him but he ought to know better than to come over here, this is Pompey territory, and we hate Southampton blokes, if they come over here we do them, if we go over there they do us, it's just the law of the land.

Back up to the front, the Action's coming on again, I must have chewed half the inside of my mouth away and my jaws ache, but that's just a brief discomfort. On they come again and the boys are really getting wild now, pointing upwards in unison, a sign of approval. I wait to see what the first number is , "In My Lonely Room" great! I'm really feeling it – beautiful but very sad, makes you want to cry.

> *"In my lonely room, my tears I don't have to hide,*
> *I know I've lost that girl, I know I love that girl*
> *I think I'll lay right down and die".*

Soon the crowd are clapping and joining in with songs like "La, la, la, la, la," the Marvelows number. Reggie King holds the mike out for the crowd to sing into it, a girl is carried out she may have fainted from the heat, or perhaps too many pills, no-one cares much anyway. The beat, the heat and the sweat carry on for about an hour, then the Action leave the stage to thunderous applause having done two encores, they look completely fagged out and they're wet with perspiration, so am I and my throat feels hoarse from shouting.

I have another coke and drop a few more pills to keep me up, then go outside where there is a great crowd of scooters revving up in the street, I join them. Girls beg lifts and a girl called Wendy asks me for one, she'll do for later I think. Old Bill shows up in force so we all move off in a crowd, weaving in and out of the traffic – some on the wrong side of the road. The girls lean back on the carriers and scream when their chauffeur has a near miss. The police keep clear they know there are too many of us, must be fifty scooters.

We're going to Bognor, where there's an allnight club, the Shoreline along the Havant By-Pass. Some of us open our scooters right up, the wind really lashes your face like a whip, still I'm doing almost seventy, not bad for two up. Then Jim Lush creams past me on big new lilac Vespa S.S., he must be touching eighty, I can see him laughing and make out I haven't seen him.

It must have been a terrifying sight to the general public now come to think of it, a great mass of scooters (and we had special exhausts to make them noisier) racing through the night at over sixty miles an hour. They were really dangerous too, I can remember having several spills myself, fortunately (for me) I never got hurt, but several blokes got killed, we would always club together and send a wreath. We never ever wore crash helmets.

The Shoreline is a sort of winding down place, I dance with Wendy for a while until I start "coming down". This is a peculiar feeling when one doesn't want to do anything except sit down and feel sorry for one's self. All around blokes are coming down sitting in rows with coffees all looking very glum. I look at the girl again but decide not to bother. A cold grey dawn is breaking over Bognor pier, and I feel dirty. It's raining, a fine drizzle, oh well might as well go home for breakfast.

26 MODS – NIK COHN

Third piece by this great '60s chronicler. Funnily enough, although Cohn wrote really well about the time, I don't think he particularly liked Mods. That said this is still a rivetting piece by a true craftsman.

Of all the teenage movements, mod is the best example of the process I spoke of earlier, by which Pop cults rise up out of the undergrowth and spread and escalate into mass-media terms, and are softened up, and then disintegrate.

It had its roots around 1960, when a few teenagers emerged as utter clothes fanatics, obsessive to a degree that had been unknown before, and that has remained unequalled since.

There were not many of them, just a few dozens scattered around the countryside. They did not run in groups, or stem from any earlier teenage style, and they were not upper-class, as almost all original dressers had been in the past. If they followed any patterns at all, they tended to come from the middle, sons of clerks and small businessmen, and a lot of them were Jewish. They were not rich but they did have enough money and security, enough remoteness from wars and depressions, to dare almost anything.

They were purists. Every penny that they had went straightaway on clothes and each detail was conceived in passion. They spent hours each morning in front of the glass, changed their underwear three times a day. In Newcastle-upon-Tyne, I knew a boy called Thomas Baines, who refused to have sex at parties unless there was a shoe-tree available and a press for his trousers.

Such figures did not become famous, simply because they called themselves by no brand-name the media could catch hold of. They weren't tangible, fell into no easy patterns and, since none of them has made a mark in other spheres and their styles never caught on generally, it is hard to choose an example. That was the point of them, in fact, that they weren't examples but existed, each of them, as individual stylists.

Nevertheless, Bernard Cautts was fairly typical. He was Jewish and middle-class by background and grew up in Southgate. When he was fifteen he left school to become a hairdresser and met a girl called Maria, who lived in Highgate: 'She was fantastic. She was so advanced and her ideas were incredible. She wore maxicoats with a fur collar, and she had dark red lips and dark eyes. She taught me everything and I woke up to clothes.'

Inspired, he went along to the offices of the *Tailor & Cutter*, the trade magazine, and thumbed through their nineteenth-century back-numbers, until he came across a Victorian frock coat, which he then had made up for himself. It was of dark grey worsted, with a double-breasted waistcoats, high buttons and flared trousers, and he wore it with a turquoise tiepin, a cravat, a stand-up Victorian collar and a gold watch, complete with chain.

At the time, he was making three pounds ten a week and this one suit alone cost £35: 'But I felt like a totally new person. When I put it on, I felt as though I was starting my life all over again.'

He progressed. Soon he was having shirts hand-made in Jermyn Street, white lawn with lace ruffles at the wrist, for ten guineas a time, and he grew his hair long in a fringe, and he haunted jumble sales, picking up tiepins, detachable shirt-collars, anything that he could find. Then he ordered a second suit, in Harris tweed, a green and brown check, made up as a hacking jacket and, when he went out with Maria and they stood together in the tube, everyone else would look amazed and move away.

'I always believed in certain values,' he says. 'Everything that I wore had to be exclusive and I could only wear a shirt once. I couldn't put on a soiled shirt and say "that's good enough", because it wasn't good enough, not for me.

'I bathed as often as I could, twice a day if possible, and I used to wash in cologne, Vent Vert by Carvin. I was never casual. Even in summer, I'd look just as good, in tweeds and waistcoats. No matter what the heat, I'd suffer, because I wanted to be perfect.

'I would have been lost without a mirror. It was my life.'

In its single-mindedness, shamelessness and snobbery, this was it the true Brummell tradition, although there was a desire to be stared at, of which Brummell would not have approved. But, in essence, Bernard Coutts and his contemporaries were genuine dandies, the first teenage exquisites. Unlike Teds or any other forerunners, they didn't wear uniforms and they didn't use their clothes for aggression, as weapons in a running battle with grown-ups. First and last, their involvement was with themselves – a true dandies' narcissism.

Because they didn't get in the papers or on TV, their influence was only local. But other kids would see them on the street, admire them and spread their message, carrying it and filtering it from neighbourhood to neighbourhood. Gradually the new attitude caught on, the notion of dressing out of self-love rather than rebellion and, by 1962, there were enough converts to make a sect, which was called Mod.

Inevitably, with the emergence of a formalized movement, the original perfectionism became a bit diluted, and most of the individualism disappeared as well. To Bernard Coutts, Mods were downright shoddy – they did not buy each item hand-made, didn't bathe in cologne. 'It wasn't what I was used to,' says Coutts. 'People used to call me Mod but I thought I was more mature. I wanted to improve myself. I couldn't just drift with the crowd.'

However, if Mods fell short of Bernard Coutts' criteria, they went far beyond anybody else's. At first they were concentrated in a few London suburbs – Stamford Hill, most notably – and they were very young, anything from fourteen upwards. Mark Feld, the infant prodigy, later Marc Bolan, Pop singer, currently successful with T-Rex, started at twelve.

'There were about seven guys living in Stamford Hill who were among the first Mods', he says. 'They were about twenty and most of them were Jewish and none of them worked. They just ponced about and lived off their parents. All they cared about was their clothes and they had new things all the time.

I thought they were fantastic and I used to go home and literally pray to become a Mod. I really did that. Then I started and gradually I came to have about six suits. Suddenly people started to look at me and come up to me and then I was accepted as a Mod.

'At this time, clothes were all that Mod was about. The music and dancing and scooters and pills came later. I'd say that Mod was mentally a very homosexual thing, though not in any physical sense. I was too hung up on myself to be interested in anyone else and, besides, I was still very young.

'I didn't think at all. The only thought I ever had was "Oh, I just bought one suit this week and I should have bought three." That was all. I was completely knocked out by my own image, by the idea of Mark Feld.'

As for the actual clothes, they changed with each neighbourhood, so that it wasn't yet possible to talk about an over-all Mod Look. Many of the jackets were updatings of the Italian style, short and boxy, and there were very tiny, elfin shoes, and Levis were more prestigious than ever. But there weren't any rules. In 1962, Mark Feld appeared in *Town* magazine, wearing a long and beautifully cut jacket, and a black leather waistcoat, a pocket handkerchief, a round-collared shirt. The effect was immaculate but unclassifiable.

Such ornateness was only possible because teenagers, during the early '60s, were in a position of unparalleled affluence. Mods could not remember the war, nor, except as a shadow, the austerity, and they were not threatened by any real poverty. When they worked, they were wealthy; even when they didn't, they collected unemployment benefit, and this cushioning produced in them smugness, a sense of power and, yes, decadence.

I do not mean that poverty disappeared. Where it survived, however, where teenagers were trapped in slums and scuffled to survive, they did not become Mods. They were ton-up boys or just plain hooligans; but Mod was a product of safety.

From the suburbs, it spread all over London, and established a new mecca in Shepherds Bush, and then swept on the south coast, and up as far as Nottingham, although it never amounted to much above the Trent; and, as it expanded, so its style diversified. Instead of existing purely for clothes, Mods became involved in music and possessions. The Rolling Stones emerged from Richmond and became the first Mod group (they were not Mods themselves but Mods adopted them and supported them) and, when they moved on to a national scale, they were replaced by the Yardbirds; 'Ready, Steady, Go!' was basically a Mod TV show; Carnaby Street, very briefly, was also Mod.

This was the Shepherds Bush era and, just as Bernard Coutts had disapproved of the first Mods, so Mark Feld now disapproved in turn. 'It began to get out of hand,' he says. 'The Mods were uncool and I wouldn't speak to them. I took it all incredibly seriously and they seemed like a travesty.'

It is true that the Shepherds Bush Mod was made of coarser stuff. Instead of creating his own look, he began to huddle in packs and he was louder, less fastidious, more physical; but scarcely less involved.

He was usually very small and solemn-looking, and about seventeen years old. He rode on a scooter and travelled in a gaggle. In every district, there would be a top Mod and, depending on how he dressed himself, that's how the whole district would dress.

In this way, Mod style varied around the country; but there were certain basic looks: little mohair suits with narrow trousers, which were pressed every day and carried around in a bowling bag, to be put on fresh before entering a party or dance hall; Ivy League jackets, in white-and-blue-striped cotton or seersucker, with long side vents; maroon or mustard-coloured suede shoes, or desert boots; army surplus anoraks, known as Parkas with bits of fox-fur sewn around the collar; knitted ties; short-legged, ankle-swinger trousers; and clip-on braces, worn beneath a jacket.

With the exception of the Parkas, which were only meant for scooter-wear, all of this was aimed at neatness and precision, because Mods were not flamboyants. They had short hair and avoided fancy dress – when Carnaby Street went riotous and tried to trap tourists with jokes, they abandoned it fast. In their tastes, they were puritan.

They were curiously self-contained. They tended not to be interested in girls, nor in anyone else. In clubs, they danced by themselves, lost in narcissistic dreams and, wherever there was a mirror, they formed queues. Often, they would wear make-up – eyeliner and mascara – but that didn't mean they were queer, or not necessarily; it was just a symbol of strangeness.

Their girls, meanwhile, camp followers, wore long fake-leather coats, suede shoes and had cropped hair and, traipsing around the boys, were ignored. They looked extremely miserable.

At weekends, the Mods came up into the West End and stayed awake for thirty-six hours. They hung around in clubs, in coffee bars and on Soho street corners and when they got tired they took pills to keep going, great handfuls of purple hearts. Apart from that, they did nothing. They seemed sexless and emotionless, passive in everything. They were not happy and not unhappy and, to the outsider, they were scary: a race of undead.

The high point of Mod undoubtedly came with the emergence of The Who, halfway through 1964, when they began to play

Tuesday nights at the Marquee Club. They came from Shepherds Bush and were Mod, or semi-Mod themselves. They were clothes-obsessives, with Union Jack jackets and Pop Art T-shirts, and a totally new outfit each for every performance, and Pete Townshend alone, their lead guitarist and songwriter, used to spend upwards of £100 a week on his clothes. He also wrote 'My Generation', which became the Mod anthem:

> *People try to put us down,*
> *Just because we get around …*
> *Things they do look awful cold*
> *Hope I die before I get old.*

By this time, Mod had been discovered by media and, from here on, the movement began to go backwards. Up till now, Mods had been something quite specific, a distinct style and approach; but now the press and TV began to use the word indiscriminately. Because Mods had once shopped in Carnaby Street, the whole Carnaby Street ballyhoo was now called Mod. After that, it was only a matter of time before anything young, anything remotely new or fashionable, was pigeon-holed Mod and, therefore, made instantly comprehensible to the general public. The Beatles were Mod; Mary Quant was Mod, and so were Marion & Franco's restaurants, and David Bailey; Anthony Armstrong-Jones was very Mod indeed. In the hands of admen, it became an all-purpose instant adjective, like Fab or Gear, to be used for Pop groups or cornflakes, or dog biscuits alike. By 1965, it had lost all meaning.

Pressured and confused by all this, thousands and tens of thousands of teenagers decided to be Mod, without ever knowing what it implied. They were just ordinary kids, a bit restless and a bit loutish, a bit bored and hot for novelty; dandyism and exquisiteness meant nothing to them whatever. 'False Mods,' says Chris Covill, a top Mod of the Shepherds Bush age. 'Just nowhere-kids who weren't dedicated. They wanted to be cool but there was violence in them and they couldn't change.'

They had none of that generic Mod self-absorption. They didn't carry their suits in bowling bags, or preen, or sit for hours in front of mirrors. Instead, they hung out in dance halls and got into fights and had sex, and they screamed into Carnaby Street, buying everything that was gaudy and cheap, while the original Mods looked on in disgust.

In reaction against Mod, meanwhile, a counter-movement had

sprung up: the Rockers.

These were ton-up boys by another name and, before Mod had come along, they had been flagging. In London, ton-up boys had declined into near-extinction and, even in the provinces, they survived only in patches, last-ditch guerrillas on motorbikes, mooching about in transport caffs.

When Mod caught on, however, there were many teenagers who refused to go along with it. Especially in the north, and in rural districts, they found it soft and creepy, and they went to the opposite extreme, butched themselves up in drainpipes and Winkle-pickers. From the ashes of Ton-up, there rose like a Phoenix the Rocker.

Most Rockers, it has to be said, were short on vocation. They were involved as a reaction against Mod, rather than out of any inner compulsion, and when Mod went kaput, so did they.

Even so, for the moment, they stuck to the rules and greased their hair, wore black leather jackets with studding and tigers embossed on the back, worshipped Jerry Lee Lewis, and battle was joined: false Mod against false Rocker.

Through 1964 and 1965, at bank holidays, they converged on towns along the south coast and clashed head-on. For forty-eight hours, there would be continuous mayhem. Then everyone turned round and went home again. While it lasted, it felt exciting, and media loved it, and it provided tailor-made material for leader writers, politicals and preachers, so that everyone was satisfied. Like the Isle of Wight pop festivals, five years later, they were perfect hype occasions – twentieth-century pantomimes, with fun for all the family.

But after the sixth or seventh successive holocaust, all roughly identical, the craze began to lose its magic. Media were losing interest, and so were the participants, particularly the Mods. The riots themselves were all right but the bits in between, all the cruising about on scooters and popping pills and the word Mod itself, seemed used up.

New styles were coming in. Marijuana was offered instead of pills, long hair instead of short, revolt instead of passivity. The ground was being cleared for hippie and, by 1966, Mod was virtually done for. From Stamford Hill to the last seaside scufflings, it has lasted less than five years, and Mark Feld was now eighteen. 'Sometimes I looked back,' he says. 'It made me feel very tired.'

27   FOLK DEVILS AND MORAL PANICS – STANLEY COHEN

Cohen was a sociologist who wrote an academic style book focussing on the Mods and Rockers shenanigans in seaside resorts. Consequently, the book is full of academic jargon but there are pieces worth wading through the text for.

The relevant setting in the Mods and Rockers case, was the English Bank Holiday by the sea and all that is associated with this ritual. A journalist who wrote that '...perhaps it is not taking things too far to look for an explanation (of the disturbances) in the character of the British weekend by the sea' was only slightly overstating the importance of such situational elements. This setting has not changed much since that particular Whitsun day described thirty years ago by Graham Greene in *Brighton Rock*. Hale had been in Brighton for three hours:

> He leant against the rail near the Palace Pier and showed his face to the crowd as it uncoiled endlessly past him like a twisted piece of wire, two by two, each with an air of sober and determined gaiety. They had stood all the way from Victoria in crowded carriages, they would have to wait in queues for lunch, at midnight half asleep they would rock back in trains an hour late to the cramped streets and the closed pubs and the weary walk home... With immense labour and immense patience they extracted from the long day the grain of pleasure: this sun, this music, the rattle of the miniature cars, the ghost trains diving between the

grinning skeletons under the Aquarium promenade, the sticks of Brighton rock, the paper saints' caps.

On the same Aquarium promenade during Whitsun 1965 I interviewed two pensioners from South London who had been coming to Brighton most of their Bank Holidays for thirty years. They spoke of the changes which were visible to anyone: people looked better off, there were fewer day-trippers and coaches, there were fewer young married couples ('all gone to the Costa Brava'), things were more expensive and – of course – there were more young people to be seen. The young were highly visible: on scooters, motor-bikes, packing the trains, hitching down on the roads from London, lying about the beaches, camping on the cliffs. But otherwise, to these old people, things had not changed much. They did not mention it, but perhaps there was one change 'for the better' compared to Greene's Brighton: there was little of the air of menace that surrounded the razor gangs and the race-course battles of the twenties and thirties.

The scene of the first Mods and Rockers event, the one that was to set the pattern for all the others and give the phenomenon its distinctive shape, was not Brighton but Clacton, a small holiday resort on the east coast of England. It has never been as affluent and popular as Brighton and has traditionally become the gathering place for the tougher adolescents from the East End and the north-eastern suburbs of London. Like Great Yarmouth, its nearest neighbour to become a scene for later Mods and Rockers events, its range of facilities and amusements for young people is strictly limited.

Easter 1964 was worse than usual. It was cold and wet, and in fact Easter Sunday was the coldest for eighty years. The shop-keepers and stall owners were irritated by the lack of business and the young people had their own boredom and irritation fanned by rumours of café owners and barmen refusing to serve some of them. A few groups started scuffling on the pavements and throwing stones at each other. The Mods and Rockers factions – a division initially based on clothing and life styles, later rigidified, but at that time not fully established – started separating out. Those on bikes and scooters roared up and down, windows were broken, some beach huts were wrecked and one boy fired a starting pistol in the air. The vast number of people crowding into the streets, the noise, everyone's general irritation and the actions of an unprepared and undermanned police force had the effect of making the two days unpleasant, oppressive and sometimes frightening.

... [At the time] much publicity was given to a special technique perfected by the Southend police [for dealing with such disturbances]. It was even quoted by a Chief Judge of the United States Court of Appeal in addressing the Chicago Crime Commission on the need for the police to get broader powers of search and seizure:

> You may have heard how the constables of Southend, England, deal with the teenage hooligans known as 'Mods' and 'Rockers' when they visit that seaside resort. Chief Constable McConnach says: 'Anything which reduces their egos is a good thing. I do not encourage any policeman to arrest them. The thing to do is to deal with them on the spot – we take away their belts. We have a wonderful collection of leather belts. They complain that they cannot keep their trousers up, but that is their problem entirely.'

...At the initial incident at Clacton,... following an incident in which twenty to thirty youths were refused service at a cafeteria, the police frogmarched two youths to the police station, with about one hundred others following behind, jeering and shouting. At 7.30 on the last evening of the Whitsun 1964 weekend, the Brighton police rounded up all the Mods and Rockers in the vicinity of the beach and marched them in a cordon through the streets to the station. This 'sullen army' (*Evening Argus*, 19 May 1964) was watched along the route by a crowd of onlookers. They were then escorted on to the train. Care was taken that no one would turn back from the first station out of Brighton: any young person with long hair or jeans had to convince the police that he lived in Brighton or Hove before being allowed out of the station. Successful symbolization provided the basis for these – and other – innovatory and dramatizing measures and ensured their support.

Such extensions of abuses of police power might be regarded by some as marginal and legitimate. Others were more serious, including allegations of wrongful arrest. In the Barker-Little sample, twenty out of the thirty-four codable answers to the question 'Why did the police arrest you?' involved charges of arbitrary arrest. These boys claimed that they had either been doing nothing or moving away from trouble when arrested. Even allowing for what is thought of as the typical delinquent response of self-righteousness, this is a fairly high proportion.

The following case is typical:

> The boy claimed that he had been playing 'childish
> games' on the beach with other Mods and came off the
> beach with a piece of wood which he had been kicking
> about on the sand. He tossed it on a pile of rubbish by
> the steps. 'A policeman said "Pick that up Eddie" and
> like a fool I did. He arrested me and I was charged with
> carrying an offensive weapon.' The boy saw that, faced
> with an apparent riot, the police needed to arrest
> somebody to deter others. He pleaded guilty in court
> because he thought it would be best to get it over with
> and was fined £75 for this and threatening behaviour
> (his first offence).

I personally observed three similar incidents and, in
addition, friends and relatives of other boys were contacted
who had stories of wrongful arrest. One such story concerned
a boy who had volunteered to go along with the police as a
witness after two friends had been arrested for throwing
stones. On arrival at the police station, despite protests, he
was arrested and charged as well. Somewhat more substantial
evidence is contained in a report prepared for the National
Council of Civil Liberties on the incidents at Brighton, Easter
1965. This was the highwater mark of police over-reaction.
Over 110 arrests were made, the vast majority of them for
offences directly or indirectly provoked by the police activity,
i.e. obstruction or using threatening behaviour. There were
very few cases involving damage, personal violence or drugs.
There was only one offensive weapon charge: a boy carrying a
steel-toothed comb.

Nine separate allegations of wrongful arrest were made in
letters to the N.C.C.L. These came from independent sources
and there is no apparent collusion. It was difficult to follow up
all these cases, but at least three resulted in successful appeal.
(In at least another fifteen cases, not known to the N.C.C.L.,
there were successful appeals for wrongful arrest or
disproportionately high sentences.) All these letters made the
same general complaint: that the police had decided in advance
to take strong measures or to arrest a certain quota and had thus
made arbitrary arrests before any offence was committed or
provoked offences to be committed. The following are extracts
from two such letters:

… a friend came up and greeted us perhaps a little louder than he should have, and was pulled aside by a police sergeant and reprimanded for doing so. While waiting for him, my friends and I were told to 'move on' by a police officer who, as he said this, pushed my friend Dave. He replied to this statement that he was waiting for our friend who was still talking to the police sergeant. The policeman then said the same thing again, still pushing Dave. 'Move on.' My friend Dave replied that he was moving on, which of course he was. The policeman told my friend not to give him any lip, my friend then asked what he had said to be lippy, the policeman then shoved my friend against a beacon by a zebra crossing saying that he had told him to move on and he was to get across there; my friend was just about to go across the crossing when a car pulled out in front of him, stopping him from crossing; the car was only there for a few seconds and within that time the policeman said to Dave, 'I told you to move, you're under arrest…' A police van pulled up and my friend was literally thrown into the van. (Letter from C.F.)

I was overtaken by a group of Rockers (25 or 30) who were walking along the pavement chanting 'Digadig – Dig' and generally behaving in a manner which I understand would be likely to frighten some people. I was not part of this group. I was not chanting, shouting or in any way behaving in a manner which did or could have frightened anyone or lead to any breach of the peace … my friend and I were merely walking to catch the train. Just as the Rockers had passed us a police van drew alongside the kerb and police jumped out of the van. I distinctly heard one policeman say: 'He will do.' I was grabbed, punched in the mouth and bundled onto a police van. I offered no resistance nor did I give any abuse – I was much too surprised at the unexpected turn of events to say or do anything. (Statement from T.M.)

T.M. and his friend, P.W., arrested at the same time, were found guilty after being remanded in custody for ten days. Later both had their appeals allowed at Brighton Quarter Sessions, one of them being awarded costs.

These reports also indicate another aspect of police activity – corresponding more closely to Cohen's 'innovation' – the unnecessary use of force. The police often used violence in handling crowd situations, e.g. by pushing and tripping young people from behind as they moved them. Force was particularly used in making arrests even when the offender had not struggled or resisted. A freelance photographer (J.G.) trying to photograph such an incident had his camera smashed and after complaining and refusing to move away, was arrested. The court was told that he was 'leading a mob of screaming teenagers across the beach' and he was charged with obstructing a constable whom he claims not to have seen till after his arrest.

Such specific claims are difficult to substantiate; observation in Brighton over that weekend, though, bears out the fact that such violence was not uncommon:

> Outside the aquarium, about a dozen Mods were brought up from the beach following an incident. The police formed a rough chain across the pavement leading to the van. As each boy was shoved into the van he got a cuff on the head from at least three policemen in the line. I also saw a sergeant kicking two boys as they were hurled into the van. (Notes, Brighton, Easter Monday, 1965, 11.30 a.m.)

A number of further allegations were made, either in the N.C.C.L. letters or to myself, involving abuses which could not be substantiated by observation as they did not occur in public. I can only say that these allegations of police misconduct after arrest were internally consistent. A repeated complaint was of the use of force in the police van – three boys writing to the N.C.C.L. claimed that they had been punched, kicked or held face downwards on the floor during the ride to the station. Every letter complained about the conditions in custody in the Brighton Police Station. Most were placed in overcrowded communal cells, together with the usual weekend drunks, from time of arrest up to anything like three days.

They were refused water or washing facilities and in one case (T.M.) given only two bread and tea meals in the twenty-seven hours between his arrest and his removal to Lewes Prison to be remanded in custody. Another boy claimed to have been given only bread and marge for forty-eight hours. All the boys, including one with a kidney complaint, whose father's representations about this were ignored by the Chief Constable and Magistrates' Clerk, had to sleep on the concrete floor. Six separate allegations were made that the police had beaten up some of the boys in the cells. The nephew, wife and mother of a twenty-two-year-old man arrested for letting down the tyres of a police van claimed to have witnessed police brutality in the station when they visited him. Another complaint, made in three letters and repeated by some of the boys in the Barker-Little sample, was that the police coerced boys into pleading guilty: 'A policeman came three times to the bars ... and made the statement that those who pleaded guilty would be dealt with sooner and more leniently, while those who pleaded not guilty would be held at least a week in remand.' (Letter from J.G.)

It should be stressed that such allegations represented very much a minority view. One of the most unambiguous of public attitudes – and one that was fed back to reinforce the actions of the police – was of support and admiration for the police. The foundation for this attitude was laid in inventory reports about 'How the Police Won the Battle of Brighton'. These reports polarised the images of the good, brave policemen with the evil, cowardly mob. The *Daily Mirror* (19 May 1964), for example, reported on how two hundred Mods advancing on the Margate Town Hall werc routed by one brave policeman. In fact, the Mods were milling around, rather than advancing and there were at least four policemen. But the counter-conceptions had to be stressed between 'The Hoodlums and the Real Heroes'; the police, self-controlled and patient, had to meet a provocative jeering mob, hundreds of whom were '... turned away by a handful of men in blue'.

These images were definitely absorbed by the public. Of the total number of post-Margate opinion statements, less than 1 per cent were critical of the police (mentioning, for example, their provocative tactics or their hypersensitivity to leather jackets or long hair). The rest only had praise for the police, or went further to make the familiar charge that the policeman's hands were tied and that he should be given more powers. In the Brighton sample, 43 (i.e. 66.2 per cent) agreed with the methods used by the police, a further 13 (20 per cent) thought that the police should have been tougher and only 9 (13.8 per cent) criticised the police for being unfair or provocative.

Additional signs of public support for the police could be seen in the courts, where prolonged applause from the public benches followed statements by the Chairman complimenting the police.

The same reaction occurred during parliamentary debates. Letters to local papers in the resorts were mainly in praise of the police, 'this gallant bulwark of society' (*Brighton and Hove Herald*, 23 March 1964). *The Hastings and St Leonards Observer* (8 August 1964) published fifteen letters about the Mods and Rockers: thirteen expressed gratitude to the police, one did not mention them and one writer complained about his son and daughter being unjustifiably harassed by the police. This last letter resulted in ten letters in the next issue denouncing the writer's attitude and accusing him of being emotional, unbalanced and waging a private vendetta against the police. These letters again expressed gratitude to the policeman '... and his allies [sic] and the magistrates'. One writer said : 'If I had a thousand pounds, I would give it to the police. What would we do without them?', and another called for money to be sent to the Police Convalescent Home '... as tangible appreciation for the police winning the Battle of Hastings, 1964'. Such calls did not go unheeded: besides the hundreds of letters sent to them directly, the Brighton police received over £100 for the Police Benevolent Fund and, according to a local journalist, were embarrassed by the sheer volume of congratulations that poured in.

28   THE SMALL FACES: THE YOUNG MODS' FORGOTTEN STORY – PAOLO HEWITT

The end is coming into view and this extract tells us why.

By the year The Beatles released *Sgt Pepper's Lonely Hearts Club Band*, the Mod movement was on its last well-tailored legs. *Ready Steady Go* was finished and the Flamingo had closed down. Once Modernism had meant sharp clothes and cool attitudes, but over the last three years it had degenerated into an unseemly morass of Bank Holiday scuffles with rockers which had been partly encouraged by media sensationalism.

The whole Mod movement looked and felt undignified. It was too large, too unwieldy and worst of all, a contradiction in terms. How can you have an elitist mass movement?

If anything summed up its downfall it was the switch of emphasis that occurred in drug culture. The choice of a new generation was not amphetamines but their counterparts LSD and marijuana.

It was the middle-class kids, the students and the drop-outs inspired by the hippie movement in San Francisco who had seized the middle ground from the Mods and imposed their new values of peace and love. Pop music changed accordingly. Especially with the arrival of *Sgt Pepper*.

Taking their cue from this obviously drug-influenced work the groups started to abandon the tight three-minute structure and explore lengthy musical avenues. One of these groups was the Pink Floyd who were often to be found at the UFO club in Tottenham Court Road playing long gigs with suitably 'trippy' light shows to augment the sound. When a Mod spotted Pete Townshend at that very same club checking out the Floyd in his flares and beads he knew for sure that an era had just died.

29   SPIRIT OF '69 – GEORGE MARSHALL

George Marshall is another dedicated soul, running his own publishing firm in Scotland. He is the author of several skinhead books and is responsible for re-issuing much of Richard Allen's work.

…Mind you, it would be a big mistake to equate the arrival of skinheads in the headlines with the birth of the cult. Fleet Street is not exactly renowned for being on the ball and this was certainly no exception to the rule. What's more, a 1968 birthdate would only add fuel to the lie that the rise of skinheads was nothing more than a reaction to the growth of the hippy movement and indeed hair in general. And we wouldn't want to do that now would we?

The word skinhead didn't come into general circulation until 1969, but kids wearing boots and sporting crops were seen in mod circles as early as 1964. They were the forerunners of the skinhead cult, which was to slowly develop from the ranks of mod from that year onwards. All the love and peace bollocks didn't come along until three years later so to argue that skinheads were somehow a reaction against hippydom is to firmly put the cart before the horse. Rejection maybe, but a reaction never.

In 1965 The Who released "My Generation", but by then the days of the mod was numbered. All the media attention that surrounded the bank holiday riots of '63 and '64 caused mod to suffer something of an identity crisis. Before, it had always been about cool, stylish kids who were one step ahead of the pack.

But now you had a massive influx of young mods who were often looked down on as "states" because they didn't have the faintest idea about class or style, and had to rely on the High Street to tell them what to wear. And of course the idea of cracking a deckchair over someone's head attracted unsavoury characters who further soiled what mod had once symbolised.

Mod was on a collision course with itself and it not surprisingly splintered on impact. Large numbers of mods had been to college and university and were influenced by the new sights and sounds around them. They joined the rag-tag army of students and hippies on the path to soft drugs, progressive rock, flowery shirts and pop art.

Thankfully, that recipe for the advancement of the cult was not everyone's cup of tea. In the north of England, for example, things were very different. Mod had began its existence towards the end of the Fifties in the clubs and cafés of London's Soho, but had taken a lot longer to catch on in the sticks north of the Watford Gap. However, the northern scene was to survive a lot longer too, centred as it was around fanatical scooter clubs and later the all-night soul dances at venues like Wigan's famous Casino Club and The Torch at Stoke.

Most importantly for the skinhead cult though, was the rise in numbers of the gang mods who stalked the urban jungles of Britain's towns and cities. Also known as hard mods, they revelled in the violent and aggressive image of post-64 modernism and began to dress accordingly. Smart suits were put away for nights on the town and fighting was done in shirt and jeans. Similarly, expensive shoes were replaced by boots which were all the better for cracking heads. And hair became shorter and shorter, as the French crew-cut came into fashion and then proceeded to go down the barber's razor scale from four to one.

London's East End was home to numerous gangs of such mods, many of whom were involved in organised crime and ended up on the wrong side of prison bars. It was certainly no coincidence that the well-dressed hoods of the London underworld were fathers, uncles, brothers or simply idols to many a mod. And those not involved liked to pretend they were anyway because it was all part of the glamour that comes from that fave mod pastime of watching too many gangster films.

In, *Youth! Youth! Youth!*, Garry Bushell talks of mods known as suits who represented, "a spartan branch of mod first spotted on the London club scene around 1965 and very much a smart, working class alternative to the dubious lure of psychedelia", and who he sees as direct ancestors of the skinhead cult. Indeed, skinheads who dressed up for a night out at the local Mecca dancehall were often called suits when the cult was at its peak in 1969 and 1970. And not just in London either.

Other cities like Liverpool, Birmingham and Newcastle boasted large numbers of hard mods, but by far the biggest concentration was to be found in Glasgow, that no mean city where gangs had been a part of growing up for every street-wise kid since the razor gangs of the Thirties and before. Glasgow's mods had always had a reputation for violence, forming themselves into Fleets and Teams (names still used by the casual gangs of today) to defend their patch of the city. Areas made infamous by these mods – Maryhill's Valley, Barnes Road at Possilpark and others – are now part of Glasgow folklore and are still given a wide berth by those of nervous disposition. In James Patrick's book, *A Glasgow Gang Observed*, one leading member of the Maryhill Young Team has a shaved head. This is 1966 and the young mod describes his haircut as "the real style", implying that it was becoming the height of gang fashion in Glasgow.

Music still played a part in the gang mods' life, but not as much as it had in the early years of the cult. There was little interest in searching out exciting new forms of music, and American soul and Jamaican ska became the staple diet for most.

Jamaican music was given a helping hand to develop in the U.K. thanks to the support of the large West Indian communities now settled here. Young white mods soon became regular visitors to the blues parties and illegal drinking holes that could be found in North Kent, Sheffield, Birmingham, Bristol and areas of London like Notting Hill and Brixton. It gave them a chance to hear the very latest sounds and this in turn brought them into regular contact with black youths. Many of these black kids had their own style of dress based on the rude boy gangs of Kingston, who had a reputation for violent clashes on the streets of their hometown. The rude boy look centred around smart suits with the trousers shortened to just above the ankle and the sleeve length to just above the wrist. This was then topped of with highly polished shoes, and often a trilby and wraparound shades.

Both mods and later skinheads were to draw on the rude boy look for style and inspiration. There is even a nice story about the Jamaican singer, Desmond Dekker, and the birth of the skinhead cult, as told by Tony Cousins. Tony ran the Creole booking agency in the late Sixties which was later to foster the successful record label of the same name.

"When we brought Desmond Dekker over we gave him a suit, but he insisted that the bottom six inches of the trousers should be cut off. Then the kids began to follow him, they rolled up their trousers and had their hair cut short."

Dekker was brought to the U.K. by Creole in 1967 to promote the single, "007 (Shanty Town)", which was a Top Twenty hit here on the Pyramid label. The Ethiopians' "Train To Skaville" (Rio), The Skatalites' "Guns of Navarone" (Island) and Prince Buster's "Al Capone" (Blue Beat) also permeated the charts that year, thanks to the massive underground support that Jamaican music was beginning to pick up at the time.

Certainly the appearance of the likes of Desmond Dekker would have helped the rude boy look travel well beyond the West Indian communities and into the wardrobes of part of this new found white audience, but there was an even bigger factor in the development of the skinhead cult besides music. And one that is often overlooked by self-styled experts on youth. Football.

England's World Cup success in 1966 had the punters flocking back to the terraces and attendance figures for all four divisions rose dramatically. Far more youngsters were attracted to the game than ever before and for the first time they went to football with their mates instead of their dads and uncles, as had been the tradition for decades before. With money in their pockets thanks to the abundance of jobs at the time, they were also able to travel to away games too – again a change to the old tradition of only going to home games.

The day of the travelling supporter had arrived in earnest and with it the opportunity to demonstrate that you were better than your opponents both on and off the pitch. Football violence had been part of the game for literally centuries, but by the late sixties it was becoming more and more organised, as rival ends went into battle on a regular basis. The terrace hooligans took on a cult status of their own, dressed as they were in heavy boots, jeans and shirt – much like the hard mod of the day who was himself no stranger to the turnstile. These were the football boot boys from whose ranks many of the first skinheads were to emerge in 1967 and 1968, and who themselves were to rise again when the skinhead cult had had its day.

From the gang mod on the street, the boot boy on the terraces and the rude boy at the dances, the skinhead cult emerged. What was at first a vague cult was given different names in different areas. Noheads, baldheads, cropheads, suedeheads, lemons, prickles, spy kids, boiled eggs, mates and even peanuts (supposedly because a scooter's engine sounds like peanuts rattling in a tin according to some observers). As late as 1969, when the skinhead had become a separate entity away from its forefathers, they were still even called mods.

Indeed anyone who doubts the mod begat skinhead story should note that Chris Welch's classic skinhead quote about, "the sight of cropped heads and heavy boots entering the midnight Wimpy bar", was actually from an article on "mods", published by *Melody Maker* in February, 1969.

By then, however, one name to describe this violent "new" youth cult was more or less beginning to stick. And the word on everybody's lips by that summer was skinhead. Even the country's Labour Prime Minister, Harold Wilson, tipped his pipe in recognition when he called certain rank and file Tories "the skinheads of Surbiton". And in no less a place than the House of Commons.

Every youth cult can be identified by the style and fashion that accompanies it, and skinhead was to prove no different. By the close of '69 a definite uniform had developed and was on display through these fair isles, but in the early days anything went that looked okay. Just as long as you had the boots you could call yourself a skinhead. And that was true of virtually every working class teenager of the day.

30 MODS – RICHARD BARNES

More from the bible, in this case to set the scene for the book's finale.

We'd just come out from the Scene to cool down a bit. It was incredibly hot and sweaty down there and we were doing the next most-cool thing, which was to hang around in Ham Yard and check each other out. The Scene club used to get pretty humid and their ventilation system consisted of a brick to hold the door open. When you first arrived, though, it was usually freezing. A lot of kids were standing around in Ham Yard in small groups talking. Half of them were pilled-up. Pete Meaden had taken about six 'blues' and was talking at everyone and clicking his fingers West Side Story-style.

It was one of those odd moments in life which you know you will remember sometime in the future. I knew that night that I would actually look back on it in years to come. It wasn't a particularly memorable night. It was exciting at the Scene Club, it usually was. There were lots of interesting new people and the D.J., Guy Stevens, the man with the best R&B record collection in the country, was playing some of his precious rare records. But I think what was memorable and struck me most that night, was that I fully realised that there existed a complete Mod way of life. I'd been involved with Mods and Mod fashions and music and been carried along by it all, but that night it hit me how all-embracing the lifestyle was, and how committed and intense everyone was about it.

I wasn't a Mod and never even thought of being a Mod. I was

at Art School. My involvement with Mods came because my friend from Art School, with whom I shared a flat, played in a group which had recently come under the co-management of Pete Meaden, and Pete Meaden, lived, ate and slept Mod. He was in the process of masterminding the group into a Mod group. I was very involved with them and so saw and experienced much of what they did at that time. Also I ran an R&B club with a friend which eventually turned into a Mod's stronghold.

The Mod way of life consisted of total devotion to looking and being 'cool'. Spending practically all your money on clothes and all your after work hours in clubs and dance halls. To be part-time was really to miss the point. It was all very new and fast and to me a bit mysterious.

The Scene wasn't licensed and only sold orange juice. It wasn't considered particularly cool to smoke or drink anyway, but we wanted a drink. So a group of us made our way down through the Soho evening crowds of Windmill Street to a pub. Mods had their own style of walking. They swayed their shoulders and took short steps, with their feet slightly turned out. It was more of a swagger, a walk of confidence. They'd sometimes have their hands held together behind their backs under their coats or plastic macs and these would sway as they bowled along. If their hands were in their pockets they would have their thumbs sticking out. That was the look. This particular night I noticed both Pete Meaden and Pete Townshend had the walk off to a T.

The small group of us swaggered into the pub. You either drank scotch and coke, vodka and lime or an orange juice. Mickey Tenner and Pete Meaden and somebody else were talking at each other so much that they never touched their drinks, although Meaden constantly picked up his scotch and coke and let it hover near his lips for a few thousand words and put it down again.

After a while Pete and I left Meaden, Mickey Tenner and the others and strolled around by Shaftesbury Avenue talking about Mods and the lifestyle. We'd been overwhelmed by Pete Meaden when we first met him. He was English but talked like an American radio disc jockey, really fast and slick. He called everybody 'Baby!' 'Hey, how are you Peter Baby, too much, what's happening, great, keep cool, can you dig it? Barney Baybee, S'nice to see you again, O.K. Baby?'

I'd never heard Murray the K or other fast talking Americans. Meaden never stopped for breath. He was like somebody you'd see in films, only he was this side of the screen, standing in front of you. He was bursting with ideas and energy and had great plans to turn the group into a cult phenomenon. The group had just got a new manager, a businessman who had a foundry that made door handles and castings in Shepherds Bush. I thought he had the idea that any businessman with the money could be a Brian Epstein. After all, managing a pop group must have seemed a lot easier than working for a fortune. Pete Meaden was hired as a publicist. He had changed their name a few months before, but he changed it once again. They were to be called the 'High Numbers'. All very Mod and esoteric. There was a lot of talk about 'Image' and 'Direction'. He was going to try to establish the group in the most important Soho Mod clubs. Meaden didn't have a lot of money, he did a bit of publicity for various pop groups for which he was poorly paid, but somehow he always looked sharp and immaculate. Quite often he would appear in a different new-looking jacket and smart trousers although he only lived in his tiny office in Monmouth Street which just had a chair, a telephone, a sleeping bag, a filing cabinet and an ironing board. He knew what was 'in' and where to get it.

This particular evening Pete and I were discussing the very point of what was 'in' and why. Meaden and Mickey Tenner and some others in the Scene club had been saying that it was time to stop wearing something or other and that such and such would be very 'hip' next week. It was incredible to me that the fashions were constantly changing, and the frequency with which they did. I wondered who thought them up. I was convinced that there was an inner clique of policy-making Mods who dictated fashion. I wondered whether they had a secret bunker beneath the Scene club, and whether Pete Meaden wasn't one of them. Now, looking back, as I knew that night I would, I realise how naive my suspicions were. However, wrong as I was, I had touched on what I suspect was a fundamental ingredient of the whole Sixties Mod thing.

I had assumed that there was a group of self-appointed Mod leaders who controlled the direction of the rest of the Mods. What I had never assumed was that the Mod 'movement' was controlled by businessmen, middle-aged plastic D.J.'s, music publishers, the CIA or the media. That's because it wasn't. The very idea, again, is to miss the point. Their entire look came from within their own undefined ranks. Apart from one or two individual journalists, the press didn't have a clue as to what was happening until the Bank Holiday riots in 1964. Up to then they weren't particularly interested anyway. The whole thing was far too mysterious for them to find it very newsworthy.

31 THE ACE FACE'S FORGOTTEN STORY: AN INTERVIEW WITH PETE MEADEN BY STEVE TURNER

The NME *interview in which Meaden brilliantly defines the Mod philosophy with the phrase, 'Clean living under difficult circumstances.' No stone is left unturned in this exhaustive but priceless piece, conducted three years before Pete tragically passed away.*

> "I'm the face baby
> Is that clear?
> I'm the face
> If you want it.
> All the others are third class tickets by me baby
> Is that clear?"
> *– Pete Meaden for The High Numbers – 1964*

Towards the end of his life Pete Meaden told me that he'd read an interview in which Nik Cohn, writer of the story that became *Saturday Night Fever* attributed the origins of the tale to his own memories of Shepherd's Bush mod society circa 1963.

In particular it was from this experience that he took the idea of 'the face', an idea which focused itself in the movie when Travolta swept into the 2001 Odyssey disco to hushed whispers and respectful glances. Travolta was The Face.

The connection Meaden was making was that if The Goldhawk Club equalled 2001 Odyssey and if The Face equalled The Face then Pete Meaden was John Travolta. The

last time something like this had happened was when The Who released *Quadrophenia* in 1973. He had listened to it and thought:

"I am Jimmy. Townshend's writing about me!"

Even if neither connection was justified, Pete Meaden deserved to feel that he was the stuff of legend. After all, it was he who saw the possibility of calculatedly making a rock group the focal point of a teenage revolution – The Who being the group, the mods being the teenage revolution. Without his style, his 'suss', it's doubtful whether The Who would carry the cultural weight they do today and it's doubtful whether Modism would have spread so far so fast.

What Meaden had was a flair for image, a love of music and a gift for gauging the spirit of the times. What he didn't have was organisational ability and a tough business edge. His shortcomings saw him virtually giving The Who's management away just as the group were making it on the strength of his ideas.

I first met Meaden in the summer of 1975 when I was researching for a book *A Decade of The Who* (Fabulous Music Ltd.). After a series of phone calls I tracked down the man nobody had heard of for years. He was a patient in a mental hospital just outside London.

Our first talk together on the 'phone got us off to a good start and resulted in the two interviews combined below – one of which took place in my flat, the other back at his room in the hospital. He'd talked to the press only once before and it was as though all the accumulated history was bursting out now he'd found someone to listen. He also seemed to feel that he'd found an opportunity to establish his role in the history of The Who.

Later I talked to Pete Townshend who admitted that there would have been no Who as we know them today if it hadn't have been for Meaden. Daltry too was quick to confirm his role. "He didn't really have to force his ideas on us very hard," he told me. "He thought we could pick up on the mod thing and he was very right because mods had no focal point at all and The Who became that, we became the spokesmen. When Kit and Chris took over management they basically just took Meaden's ideas and made them bigger.

I saw a lot of Pete Meaden during the three years following our interview. It was a time during which he pulled himself together after years of drug abuse, a nervous breakdown and a divorce. He got back into the music business co-managing The Steve Gibbons Band along with Who manager Bill Curbishley. A decade or more after The High Numbers here he was back again in The Who camp.

The last time I saw him was in June 1978 when he came along to hear me read my poetry at a small theatre club in Waterloo. He was full of smiles but there was a vacancy behind it all. We went for a drink and his conversation was disjointed, abstract. All I can remember now are some apocryphal visions of the end of the world and some questions about religion; "Who's the one then – Maher Baba or Jesus?"

Within a month he was found dead in bed of barbiturate poisoning. He was thirty-six and back living with his parents in the home where he'd dreamed up The High Numbers and written 'I Am The Face'. The coroner passed an open verdict although close friends feel that Meaden knew too much about drugs to die of a careless mistake.

It seemed a very mod place to die, a cramped terraced house in an Edmonton cul-de-sac and also a very mod way to die. Before his death he'd been feeding in ideas to the writers and producers of *Quadrophenia*. I think he would have liked the result but I can't imagine him being more than amused at the mod revival; the spirit of Modism was after all so much against recreating the past. Modism was pushing forward.

Where do we begin?

Existing is what it's all about because with society as we know it breaking down, I think that survival is of the utmost importance. It's all very well being immensely talented, having a good time and making great music – but not being able to sustain it. This sustaining bit is the most important of all and The Who are survivors. That's what I'm interested in, what I've always been interested in. There was a long period of time when The Who didn't have any hit records at all, but their music is survival music by the pure power of sustaining – sustaining power – that's what you have to say about The Who. This is what I built on in the very first place; I say I because I think nobody's had more effect on their career, as I did, in putting together The High Numbers. I met them with a guy called Bob Druce and another feller called Helmut Gordon. Bob Druce was an agent who booked them and he said he had a contract on The Who in his desk. I was introduced to The Who by my barber via a friend of mine who was a mutual friend called Phil The Greek. Phil The Greek was later to appear on television on *Ready, Steady, Go!* with a loaded sawn off shotgun, you know? He was one of the great legends of folk lore and pop history.

Do you think the Mod thing is still alive?
I wonder actually where all the old Mods went – they're probably all in garages, second-hand car outfits, scrap-yards, something like that. 'Cos there's such a thing as Mod Suss – you know – sussing out a situation. That's what Mods are about – suss out a situation immediately, its potential, controlling it. Rather than letting the potential control you. So I would think they'd get in the car game – that's where most money is made very quickly.

Are you in touch with any of your old mates?
Yeah, one's a coke-dealer, one's in prison and another one's the guy who appeared on television with a shotgun with The Who on *Ready Steady Go!* who was the greatest Mod leader of them all – Phil The Greek. Pete Townshend and I talk about him often.
The black girls are Mod chicks of today – those little spade chicks you see running round in stacked heels and wedges wearing sort of Ossie Clarke clothes. The blacks were always there in 64, there weren't so many of them – they were late-night kids like us – you'd go out on a three-day bender, you know? Hit out on a Friday night high on speed down to *Ready Steady Go!*, down to the Scene Club, dance all night till Saturday morning, Saturday you'd go shopping to buy a pullover or scarf or something – pair of socks, 'cos your feet hurt, dancing all night in Desert boots, and then all through Saturday night again at the Scene Club all through to Sunday morning, that's when the come-down comes down, 'cos you can't sustain it much more than three days, two nights. Three days and you start heading home to Mama's place you know? 'Cos you live at home, you can't afford to live anywhere else apart from Mama's place, and then you crash, round about Sunday morning, if you can get a lift home to North London, where I was. And that was the life – it was the most amazing sort of life you could imagine – it was so amazing.

What do you mean when you say you 'got The Who together'?
I got them together, in that I loved the life so much, I got The Who and I dressed them up in Mod clothes, gave them all the jingoism and all the paraphernalia of Modism, boxing boots and

fashionable things, right on the button, timing just right, 'cos timing is where it's at, you know?

You were already a Mod, by then?
Yeah, I was a Mod, it was my life. There was a little club called the 'Scene Club', just at Ham Yard, off of Great Windmill Street, and there, on several nights a week the greatest records you can imagine were being played. There were records like 'Ain't Love Good, Ain't Love Proud' by Tony Clarke, Major Lance's stuff, Smokey Robinson, early Curtis Mayfield's Impressions stuff, you know, which was eminently danceable by people who were not emotionally involved with other people. There was a lack of women in those things, I mean we all dig women, but if you're in the West End, you know that you pay for your women, and well, you don't get them, 'cos the girls that come up are mysteries, right. You get the girls that come up and dance around, little girls that just dance around in the pubs, just having a little dance around, just having a little groove. The records were played very loud over those big speakers, like fairground speakers, and in a small room, which was what the 'Scene Club' was, with concrete walls, so it comes bouncing back, hitting off the floor – there was no wooden-floor, hits off the ceiling, so you're getting saturated with sound, and then they start pulling down all the stops, you're getting a psychedelic record in '64. So you're picking up on the body all the time, this is what Mods are about, they're very physical people. Drynamil is a drug for Mods, because it's a functional drug, it's a drug you can work on, you can steal in the shops on it, do all the things you need to do, you can dance on it – you lose all lack of confidence, you lose guilt. It opens up the capillary vessels in the body; so you become aware of your system, become aware of your body, therefore, with the aid of this drug you have your own society, you have Nirvana in a single little purple pill. Plus you got good togs, which is your clothes, you have the confidence, plus you have the sustaining power three days up, two nights up. I think it's a groove, I think it's fabulous, man!

When did you first notice all this happening?
When my doctor gave me Drynamil for anxiety. She gave me the original Drynamil, the original Purple Hearts. And I went back that night to my place, my parent's house where I was working from, and I got out the pills and I took one, it was just like medicine, you know, it doesn't do anything. It's probably

doing something physically way down in your system and you don't notice it. Then suddenly Bang! I was free! I was unburdened by chains of resistance. I was able to write and draw and do all the things I wanted to do, without the restraints of normal civilisation bothering me, like feeling it's late, and having to go to bed. It was all just as simple as that. I sat up all through the night, and finished the book in that one night.

Were pills very popular then?
No, well this is how I discovered them. This was 1962 actually.

So the Mods weren't in existence then?
No they weren't in existence, but Jack Kerouac was. So anyway, I took the Drynamil. I finished the book in a night, and I was up for three nights trying to wear my energy off. My own personal feeling is that the debt you have to pay for drugs is too much to compensate for taking the drug in the first place, I always say don't take any drugs whatsoever. A few smokes, a few beers, speed a little bit now and again, be careful with anything else. That's all.

Did you sort of think that you were the King Mod at the time?
No. I was the feller who saw the potential in Modism, which is the greatest form of life-style you can imagine – it's so totally free – totally anti-family London – in so much as that there were lonely people having a great time. Not having to be lonely, not having to be worried about relationships, being able to get into the most fantastic, interesting, beautiful situations, just out of music. You could dance by yourself, you could groove around. I saw this as a weekend. I mean, imagine this, on a Friday night I would go down to *Ready, Steady, Go!*, groove around there, and one weekend I had three people on there, I had The Crystals, Chuck Berry and The Rolling Stones – doing publicity for those three people. They used to say, 'The Weekend Starts Here' and the weekend would begin there, I would take my speed and go down there, I would go up to the Green Room, and watch my people, that I was working for having a great time on the television. There'd be all the faces and people that I knew. A face is just someone you recognise, you might not even know his name, but he's known as a face.

That's why you called it 'I Am The Face'?
Yeah, 'I Am The Face' is one of the people who is familiar.

Ready, Steady, Go! was interesting in so much as it got the vibe right out, with the right amount of grit edge on it. It was no good trying to get in through the doorman, 'cos there was always so many kids outside trying to get in as well, so you had to thrust your way through that with a lot of hard chat, into the main foyer at ATV House, down there in the Strand, and then you go downstairs into … oh you go into the Green Room first, and you have a few sherberts to round the edge off the Drynamil, and then down into *Ready, Steady, Go!* and there was Mickie Tenner and Phil The Greek dancing around with some of the girls and there'd be Sandy Sargent, who is Mickie Tenner's wife now, and Cathy McGowan, and there'd be the Stones around, or The Who or Paul Jones, Manfred Mann and that would be a great foot for the weekend to start off on. That would be a nice edge, like the kickstart on a motorbike – kick it WHOOMP and she starts firing, and you go off into the weekend.

You didn't sleep at all?
No, you didn't sleep at all – you stayed up all night.

You saw The Who becoming a focal point for all this?
Yeah, they were the focal point, because I was thinking about revolutions then, I was thinking about society was great when you had speed, a couple of pints of cider, listen to the music and you can be completely enveloped in music, sounds, and if you could add the visual impact of a really tough group, which was what I wanted, then you had The Who, you had the High Numbers in fact, you gotta remember that and not forget. It was known as the High Numbers and that was the focal point of Mod-dom.

Tell you what we never got onto, when you met The Who?
Yeah, I was … a friend of mine called Phil The Greek who was the flashiest Mod that I knew, he was the Mod Leader, in so much as that he wore a dark blue suit, mohair suit, and he used to come down with me to the Scene Club, and we used to go to the same barber called Jack.

Did he do some good Mod-cuts?
No, he was just a barber, who would do what you wanted him to do, like how barbers should be. Not like the guy up at Crimpers or something, saying how he thinks your hair should be. Now if you go to those Jewish barbers they do your hair just

right, as you ask him. Jack said to me that he knew of a group that was interesting.

Some months before that I'd been thinking out very seriously of how I could get the focus, or the focal point for my feelings and the feelings of mods who used to go to The Scene. The Club was owned by Ronan O'Rahilly of Caroline fame, at the time, but it was run by a feller called Lionel Blake. Now that was the real hard core fashion situation, system, call it what you will, position of glory if you like, because I used to go down there, it was very private, if you danced yourself to the music, which was new wave R&B.

I was taking pills, in so much as I'd been introduced to pills by my doctor for the anxiety thing, while I was a graphic designer for John Michael, the clothes shop. I took some Drynamil, and it kept me up for three days, and I zoomed around on that – I had such a great time, fabulous time. I would go out with ten bob in my pocket, and my doctor's pills from the National Health, which didn't cost anything in those days I think, she would give me thirty a month, Purple Hearts, the triangular ones with the line down the middle. So anyway I was living this lovely life of Riley, where I was just listening to the music I liked, which was very private – I didn't have to get hung up on birds – early Mods never did. Well, they used to go out with birds down at the Tottenham Royal. I used to down to the Scene Club, and there it was very private, very dark. I used to down there with Brian Jones, and Chuck Berry I took, a few people like that. The Animals used to play there, but none of that was exactly purism Mod – which was a society unto itself. As I say, Modism, Mod living is a euphemism for clean living, under difficult circumstances. You have your own values, your own set of time scales, your own units of existence, which are to have a good time, because it's alright, as the old Curtis Mayfield Impression song goes.

I'd been knocking around with The Rolling Stones, Andrew Oldham, the manager of The Rolling Stones, who had Andrew Logan, and I was his first business partner in a company called 'Image'. We were doing things, and I went to Spain for seven months, came back from Spain, I met the Stones on my first morning back, they were recording 'Come On' and 'Money', at Decca, West Hampstead. I saw Andrew in the studio, pushing up the control knobs on the deck there, all I could see him doing was bringing up bass lines, and the high treble on the top end of the guitar line, and putting Mick's voice forward, and there was Bill there. He had a great pair of trousers – they were stove-pipe trousers, which I was very much impressed by, 'cos I was very much into clothes. Anyway, so I knocked around with the Stones, and I used to go to their early gigs, and in fact, I lived with Mick for a little while, in Cricklewood, bordering on Kilburn – you can't get much worse than that, as a bedsitter-land, because nothing happens out there, I can tell you. Anyway, I sussed out what the Stones were about, and their appeal, and I saw for the first time in my life, all those little girls screaming at them, and they were just playing their R&B stuff, none of the Booker T. or the Georgie Fame trip, but just doing real good R&B and there was Mick up there in his gilly jacket but the collar wasn't right anyway. Andrew was making fortunes then, you see, I was doing publicity for people I liked, like Chuck Berry.

So the Stones played down at the Scene Club?
Oh yeah. I used to go down there with Brian Jones, who was a very close friend of mine, he liked to groove around, he used to come down with his snakeskin boots on and his regency stuff and the high scarf and that – regency collars. He'd come down to the Scene Club, and I used to wear Ivy League, which is Canadian-cum-American Esquire Ivy League Jackets – natural shoulder line, you know? I'd groove around in my desert boots, bop around, listen to the music, and Brian came down, and he was top Super Star number 1, coming up fast, and he felt out of place in the Scene Club, it was so clique-ish, so highly identified with themselves. And he was with the hippest, heaviest outfit in the world coming up which was the Stones, if they didn't fit in, that meant that something was going wrong somewhere.

You say Mods weren't into chicks?
Not too heavily into chicks, no, because chicks you got to remember are emotional distressful situations for a man, and we were totally free because your sex drives, your libido, I think it's called your libido, was turned right down low, well I…

You took them down the Scene Club?
I took them down the Scene, went down there, had a look around, and I said 'Look, you can't go wrong… Why don't we become the focal point, the focus, the brand new feel, of music and lifestyle?
We went down to Welwyn Garden City, and I remember what actually happened was that I said 'Listen, we've got to do a

record, and we've gotta do it fast. I haven't got much money, and haven't got much time, in so much as I don't know who's supposed to be manager, but I think I'm supposed to be managing. I'm taking over responsibility for this. I took responsibility for The Who – that's what I'm saying now.

What was their reaction to the Mod scene?
Well, Pete identified immediately – we went down to Austens and had the jacket made. Yeah, I worked very hard on The Who, The High Numbers…

I used to lie in my bed, in my single bed at my parent's place in Edmonton, and think Name – name. WHO? World Health Organisation. Well that's alright, but it's too abstract, it's too ethereal, too airy fairy to connect with me. Now if it was called the World Health Organization and that's good, but I want a name that is adaptable, that is going to sustain more than just six months. I put this brochure together which was completely Mod, without any help from their so-called manager and was asked to become their manager. I was manager of The Who and I put it together like, whoever wants to say it about them, the Mods are what The Who are all about. It was pithy, as euphoristic as you can get, and that is what I'll say right now. Can you turn this tape off?

Why?
I'm getting angry now, in so much as, well not only in the sense of anger, but realisation is coming upon me to say, where I got the suits right, and I got the cycling jackets just right and the T shirt under that, the boxer boots on, the jeans, the Levi's with the one-inch turn-up so the inner seam just showed out, from the outside, and Pete's jacket was right on, with the top button just done up, and they went up the Railway Inn at Harrow, Wealdstone. I was the one who went up to Kit Lambert and said 'Listen, man, this is the heaviest group you have ever seen, give us a gig, 'cos I'm hustling for my boys. They're my mates, and whether you like it or not, I'm doing my thing here!' I gave him the handout which said 'Four Hip Young Men From London', who say *I'm The Face*, and wear Zoot Suits.

'The first authentic Mod record'. Well, that was my trip, I did that entirely myself, off my own back. Nobody helped me, nobody encouraged me, but I laid it on you, on your Kit and on Pete.

When did you write 'I Am The Face'?
I wrote it on the morning of early '64 … it came from Guy

Stephen's record collection. There was a record called 'Got It If You Want It' by Slim Harpo, an R&B musician, who didn't make much money, as I found out when he died recently. He used to get paid in wine. Anyway, I took the instrumental track, I can't hold a tune in my head.

What about 'Zoot Suit'?
'Zoot Suit' was the fashion record of all time – it pinched the backing track of 'Country Fool' by The Showmen, which was the B-side of 'It Will Stand'. The Showmen are now known as The Chairmen of The Board and 'It Will Stand' is the rock'n'roll tribute anthem of all time. I heard the melody, and the night before the session I dreamt up the lyrics, and I wrote them all down – I wrote them down on speed. The actual words were 'I'm the the hippest number in town, And I'll tell you why' and it goes into 'I wear a Zoot Suit jacket with side-vents 5 inches long' and it's a great song man …

Did the Mods catch onto it?
Yeah of course they did, it was a fashion song. I bought 250 copies off the record company, off Fontana, to get it into the charts and I used to take them round myself. I worked so hard at it man.

Did it get in the charts?
No, but it got so many plays that I got £112 – I don't know how many pence you get for each play, but there was quite a few plays.

Townshend wasn't writing at this time?
No he wasn't.

What sort of music were The Who playing?
DeTours' covers – The DeTours were an R&B band; 'The Who' was Pete Townshend's song …

No original material whatsoever?
No. They were playing a little bit of Bob Dylan, but mostly Beatles records and R&B. When I met them I said 'You gotta play mod music', which was new wave R&B – all the time man, all the time right on. Classics like 'Ain't No Good,' 'Ain't No Proud'. 'Have To Dance To Keep From Crying' was one of the records I was doing with them.

So, by this time, are The Who becoming the focal point?
Yeah, and the mods would talk about them. I got them the residency, and then Tuesday nights things would start picking up you know? The Who were real Mods now I'd changed them because all a Mod is is having self-respect.

Did they wear the Mod clothes offstage?
Yeah I told them to. I bought the jacket for Roger, I mean, the jacket was the high point of my career.

Did you make them get their hair cut?
Yes, of course I did, I took them down to Jack the barber.

Was there ever any feeling that you'd made them do it as a commercial exercise?
Yeah, I think Roger felt this way, perhaps, but John … I don't know about John. He said he didn't want to wear the clothes, and went through a puddle in his boxing boots.
Yeah, well, you see, I knew it was right on, how can you deny a fact of something smack bang in your face man: 'This is where it's at, this is what we're doing. Please do it, we're gonna become a success, we can't help it, and then you can be my mates as well.'

There must have been a point where the band – I mean I've read interviews with The Who where they say – it was about '64 – saying 'We Are Mods' right, there must have been a point where they suddenly decided they were Mods?
Yeah, but Mods is a … like I went down to Hastings, in '66…

What – to kill a few Rockers?
There weren't any Rockers, there were just Mods, that's how overpoweringly successful the whole trip was – there was something like 15 thousand Mods down there, and there were three rockers in a cafe – three. There were two down the road in another cafe, or sitting around on their bikes, and the Mods came down, it was so beautifully succinct.

How did you lose The Who?
Well, I wasn't too hip in business – trips in the music business … Kit Lambert came round that night at the Railway Inn in Harrow, Wealdstone, and he came up to me, he lied to me, he said he was a promoter looking for a band, to put in his club, so I

gave him the hard-sell: 'This is absolutely where it's at. You cannot fail on this squire,' I said. 'If you'll just listen to me, you can make a lot of money out of this, as promoter, because they are of the people, they are the hippest numbers in town, there's no-one quite like them. Just look at that queue down there.' And so I hard-sold myself right out of a band.

What happened?
Kit came back to me, anyway, I tried to get in touch with Pete for a few days, but strange things were happening. Pete didn't answer his phone – he wasn't at home. Then Roger said, 'We're going with this feller – let's go and have a drink.'

So they approached you independently?
Well, Roger was the leader of the band, so Roger and I went and had a drink in a pub in Brewer Street, and I bought him a drink, and he said, 'Well, listen man, we're gonna get paid £20 a week, now, and plus our cars, why don't you go and have a talk with Kit?' He came out straight with it, and there was nothing more to say about it, except Kit got in touch with me and said, 'Let's have lunch.' I think it was probably Pete said, 'Look after him' or something, 'cos I'm a fragile person, you know?

You didn't have a contract with them?
Yeah, I had a contract with them.

So did Kit buy it, or what?
No, I just signed over any rights I had for them for the first figure he gave me. So I figured if that's what my mates want to do, then that's what they have to do. Maybe in the future they'll look after me – 'cos I need looking after in this life – I need looking after.

And did you continue your friendship after the splits?
Yeah – after the split, Kit Lambert took me into a restaurant which I worked in, as a matter of fact, where I worked for three days, when I was much younger, to learn how to carve onions. And Kit said, 'How much do you want?' and I said, 'I don't know how much I want, Kit, I don't know what sort of value you put on it'. I was frightened out of my life, because I'd made a monster, I knew it was a monster, and he said, 'I'll give you £500 for them'. I learnt later that I was supposed to accept £5,000 but I just said. 'Yeah, that's alright, that'll do – thanks a lot.'

Still, least he was honest enough, and didn't just rip them off me. So he sent me something like £145, or £142 or something, in various sums, and a couple of weeks later I went down to Brighton … here's my band, playing in the Aquarium, Brighton, and I couldn't even bloody go in and see them, man – there were too many fucking Mods about, the whole of the South Coast was turning into the Mods, right away. I mean, I'd done publicity, I'd got them into every single magazine you can possibly imagine – I'd made The High Numbers the hippest number in town …

Did you keep the cuttings?
Yeah, I kept them, but I threw them away after a while.

Was the Scene Club still operating?
Well, it closed down about 1966.

In your opinion, when did the Mod thing phase out?
About 1967, when Acid came in.

You think Acid phased it out?
Yeah.

What about … 'cos you get these styles, and you develop out of it don't you? Did it sort of burn itself out, or what?
Well, I was with Beefheart then, I had Jimmy James and the Vagabonds from 1965.

Yeah, I was talking about music, I was talking about clothes.
I was into continental clothes, Curtis Mayfield clothes…

What do you think was the ultimate Mod kit?
Tonik jacket, blue jeans, or tonik trousers in a different colour…

That's jacket and trousers?
Jacket with about a seven or eight inch centre-band, and … it's a starfish quality cloth, and it's tight – you wear tight sleeves, tight shoulders, and a comfortable jacket, you know, with a centre-band. It was straight enough to be drape, and small enough to be tight enough, and you just did the top, button up, and then you'd have a pair of tonik trousers of a different colour, probably blue and bronze, straight down, but widish, hipsters. You'd have your belly-button showing, with a french

jersey, with a crew neck on it, and then you'd have a Mod scarf, with a single twist in it so it flies out on both sides. A pair of desert boots, and you're set for the weekend. Or if you got a scooter, you got a pair of dark glasses, maybe a stingy brim hat, with an inch-wide brim, or else a pair of dark glasses, and then an anorak, and then you sit on your scooter, and you'd have everything, even your sleeping-bag, which is your anorak, Parka, yeah ...

What about your haircut?
French crew – razor-barbered, you know there was no lacquer, it was blow-dried, it was called the College-boy, short at the sides 'cos you're mostly blond, like fair-haired geezers, they all seemed to be – don't know why. You didn't have too many whiskers – like that Samuel Palmer picture you know? He hasn't got too many whiskers !

Some of the Mods got into make-up, didn't they?
Not really, they could have done, but that's because effeminists got into it.

Did you ever hear about Mods using make-up?
Yeah, I heard about it man, but when you're out for four days on the trot man; you don't listen about make-up. All you're doing is trying to have a good time, and try to keep yourself clean, you know?

Were there ways of walking?
Yeah, you walked speedwise, which is like, you put both hands in your Mod jacket. Of course, your head's bent against the wind, so you got your head down, talking left to right, and peeking left to right.

Was there a way of smoking?
Yeah, you smoke it as cool as you like, man, and you're smoking king-size.

What, inside your hand?
No, it's never covered. You drink black coffee, cup of french, you know? You'd be on french brews, and you smoke, as cool as you can be, you know? And you drink french brews, just to keep your system down, 'cos you've been up for three nights already and your stomach's starting to rise.

Did Mods read?

They'd read things of knowledgeable interest like William Burroughs, I reckon, if they ever got on to William Burroughs, to find out what new drug trips were all about – information on drugs … practical things.

What was the Mod revolution all about then?

My Mod revolution was an undefined revolution against commodities and people. That is people were commodities, my parents treated me as a commodity, and Modism to me was a release, sweet release, relief. The burdens of mundane existences and I had, personally had something like 250 thousand Mods running around the South Coast, South of England.

Did you go to the big fights?

Yeah I went to some of the big fights. I saw them.

What was it like?

Just too many of us and none of them – we overpowered them – like ZAP!

What sort of feeling did you get, actually being involved?

There was no focal … no focus … The Who were letting us down, they should have been there with us, they should have been there, THEY SHOULD HAVE BEEN THERE WITH US!

You must have felt elated…

Yeah, I was elated when I was there, like seeing fifteen thousand kids, all on the street with you, with exactly the same clothes – I was with Bob Bedford, who's now a millionaire insurance broker, and he was a Mod same as me, he used to work on a music paper, and we went out in '67, down to Hastings – I knew it was over. I knew it was falling apart, but I went down there because I wanted to see what the riots were about. I had my own Mod band, which was the Vagabonds, There should have been a conscious effort on the part of the Who to stick with the Mods, not to go into Pop art or those things, because Pop art was not where it's at.

Did the Mods follow the pop art?

No they did not. They never did, you can never say that about the Mods. That was a sell-out on The Who's part. I'm not being bitter now, but it was my revolution, I had 250 thousand people on my side – in uniform, fighting for something which, was clearly defined to me …

Would you say 'My Generation' was a Mod song?
'Course it was. It was a pride factor, on Pete Townshend's part, to talk about … No I don't think he was too much into Jagger or anything like that, but he was talking about … more about pop stars, songs, like Dylan, Lennon and Jagger, people …

He was turning on to them?
Yeah, 'course he was getting turned onto them – they were his friends, they were my friends as well, Jagger was my friend, and I was Dylan's first publicist.

When do you think that The Who lost their grip on the Mod market?
'67, easy, maybe before that.

While they were doing the Pop art stuff they still had the Mod clothes, as well?
I'm not letting down The Who, I'm just saying that I've gotta draw a perspective of what the situation was. The situation was, that here was a huge group of people, well the market, I tend to call them markets 'cos … well, I try to be humane about it, human in so much as the Mods were, for me, the revolution, the revolutionary group, they're like the VietCong out in Cambodia, you know The VietCong. There's a North Vietnamese army who are stolid troops, and there's the VietCong who are like Mods, who are the ones who've been fighting all the time. They've never let down the side, they've never come in in strength, they've always been fighting in a minority group, against the vast armour of the American army.

What did you think of Quadrophenia? *[Ed's note: the album, not the film]*
Brilliant, it's … I identified with it entirely, 'cos Jimmy could easily be Jimmy of Jimmy James and the Vagabonds. He's talking about a Mod, well, I am a Mod, the Mod who made Mods out of The Who.

When did you feel The Who let you down, as representing Mods?
When I never got that ticket at Brighton Aquarium, that night, when I saw fifty thousand kids queueing up down there.

The mod thing was style as opposed to content, wasn't it?
Yeah, in as much as you can dismiss life as having no substance, there was no substance. But if you can put life together as having substance, a reason to believe, then you have Modism, which is where it was, which was via having a pill, having a few drinks, via having music to listen to, and a style of your own, so succinctly beautiful and self-contained, where privacy was everything, and no-one ever disturbed your privacy, because you are all the same ...

It takes a structured society to support that kind of thing?
Yeah, you have to stretch society, that's why they had policemen walking around...

I mean, it takes a structured society to support that kind of thing, I mean everybody couldn't be a Mod, because...
No, anybody can become a Mod, that's the beauty of it, anyone can become a VietCong ...

Can you imagine 20 million people staying out every weekend?
That's what my dream was.

But, who would do the work?
They did work because they worked during the day-time, you gotta understand this ...

Well what about Nurses ... nurses can't be Mods, can they?
'Course they can, they're the best Mods of all...

What if they're on night duty?
Well, they'll come out in the daytime, go shopping with you, and they'll have the short haircuts, and nurses are about the best Mods of all, because they're actual practical people. Can't you understand, that's what Mods are all about.

When did you stop being a Mod?
I stopped after Acid came in ... I used to call myself a Black Tripper.

So you were into a Hip thing?
No, no, Hippies wore flowers, I had the Allie Kans jacket, a £300 jacket ...

And when did all that come out...?

Well, that was when I brought Captain Beefheart to Great Britain... I had my mental breakdown, my nervous breakdown...

Was that a result of your old hard-living, do you think?

Yeah... I'd done three and a half years on the road with Jimmy James and the Vagabonds, which the purist Mods...they weren't believing me anymore, and I was feeling that the structure is breaking down, and Modism – Modism has to be sustained up and it has to be a rigid, rigorous structure for Modism to function in it.

Do you think that The Who eventually became Mods or at least Pete and Roger, or something ...

I think Pete is the greatest Mod of all time ... and myself.

Were you interested in them being Mods, or just appealing to the Mod market?

No, I made them into Mods, and they weren't Mods, they were ... they have always said they were never Mods ... I made them like ... it's just saying, they're my best mates, and if I can't make my mates into the best mates you can ever make, mates you can be proud of, then I cannot do anything for my friends, then if they go off for ten years or something, I've still kept in touch with them, but if they go off for ten years ... all I can say, all it was, as I said to Pete Townshend on the telephone, I only made you into The Who, because I wanted you to be my mates.

A NOTE ABOUT THE EDITOR

Paolo Hewitt is the author of six acclaimed books including his latest, *Forever The People: Six Months on the Road with Oasis* (1999, Boxtree). He is also responsible for wearing immaculate loafers in the offices of *NME* whilst discovering Hip-Hop and Acid House for them, and for coining the phrase, 'Never read your own press, weigh it.'

Paolo still lives in London where he maintains a beautiful pair of eyes.

Available Now From Helter Skelter Publishing

Bob Dylan by Anthony Scaduto 1-900924-00-5 £11.95
The first and best biography of Dylan.

"Scaduto's 1971 book was the pioneering portrait of this legendarily elusive artist. Now in a welcome reprint it's a real treat to read the still-classic Bobography".
Paul Du Noyer, Q***

"Superb on the Greenwich Village scene, insightful on the meaning of John Wesley Harding ... it's still perhaps the best book ever written on Dylan".

A Journey Through America With The Rolling Stones by Robert Greenfield   1-900924-01-3 £12.00
Definitive insider's account of the Stones' legendary 1972 US tour.

"Greenfield is afforded extraordinary access to the band... drugs... groupies. In all, it's a graphic if headache inducing document of strange days indeed".
Tom Doyle, Q**

"Sure, I was completely mad. I go crazy."
Mick Jagger

Back To The Beach - A Brian Wilson and the Beach Boys Reader edited by Kingley Abbott 1-900924-02-1 £12.99
A collection of the best articles about Brian and the band, together with a number of previously unpublished pieces and some specially commissioned work. Features Nick Kent, David Leaf, Timothy White and others with a foreword by Brian.
*"A detailed study and comprehensive overview of the BB's lives and music. Most impressively Abbott manages to appeal to both die-hard fans and rather less obsessive newcomers."***Time Out**
"Rivetting!" **** **Q Magazine**

Born In The USA - Bruce Springsteen and the American Tradition by Jim Cullen 1-900924-05-6 £9.99

The first major study of Bruce Springsteen's that looks at his music in the context of his blue collar roots, and his place in American culture

"Cullen has written an excellent treatise expressing exactly how and why Springsteen translated his uneducated hicktown American-ness into music and stories that touched hearts and souls all around the world." **Q****
"This is a provocative look at one of America's cultural icons." **Newsweek**

Available Now From Helter Skelter Publishing

New Titles From SAF Publishing

Wish The World Away - Mark Eitzel and the American Music Club
by Sean Body ISBN: 0 946719 20 9
192 pages (illustrated) UK £11.95

Mark Eitzel's songs are poignant, highly personal tales, encapsulating a sense of loss and loathing, but often tinged with a bitter twist of drink-fuelled humour. Through his solo work and that of his former band American Music Club, Eitzel has been responsible for some of the most individual and memorable records of recent years. Through unrestricted access to Eitzel, former band members, associates and friends, Sean Body has written a fascinating biography which portrays an artist tortured by demons, yet redeemed by the aching beauty of his songs.

LUNAR NOTES - Zoot Horn Rollo's Captain Beefheart Experience
by Bill Harkleroad with Billy James   ISBN: 0 946719 217
160 pages (illustrated) - UK £11.95

Bill Harkleroad joined Captain Beefheart's Magic Band at a crucial time in their development. Beefheart rechristened Harkleroad as Zoot Horn Rollo and they embarked on recording one of the classic rock albums of all time - *Trout Mask Replica* - a work of unequalled daring and inventiveness. Further LPs, *Lick My Decals Off Baby* and *Clear Spot*, highlighted Zoot's skilled guitar playing and what a truly innovative band they were. For the first time we get the insider's story of what it was like to record, play and live with an eccentric genius such as Beefheart.

Meet The Residents - America's Most Eccentric Band! by Ian Shirley
ISBN: 0946 719 12 8   200 pages (illustrated) UK £11.95
Fully updated and now available again!

An outsider's view of The Residents' operations, exposing a world where nothing is as it seems. It is a fascinating tale of the musical anarchy and cartoon wackiness that has driven this unique bunch of artistic maverics forward.

"This is the nearest to an official history you are ever likely to get, slyly abetted by the bug-eyed beans from Venus themselves". **Vox**
"Few enthusiasts will want to put this book down once they start reading".
Record Collector

Digital Gothic - A Critical Discography Of Tangerine Dream
by Paul Stump   ISBN: 0946 719 18 7
160 pages (illustrated) UK £9.95

In this critical discography, music journalist Paul Stump picks his way through a veritable minefield of releases, determining both the explosive and those which fail to ignite. For the very first time Tangerine Dream's mammoth output is placed within an ordered perspective.

"It focuses fascinatingly on the pre-soporific roots of the group and their place in a cool electronic lineage which traces right up to Detroit techno". **Mojo**
"A stimulating companion to the group's music". **The Wire**

Available From Firefly Publishing

an association between Helter Skelter and SAF Publishing

**Poison Heart - Surviving The Ramones by Dee Dee Ramone
and Veronica Kofman   ISBN: 0946 719 19 5
192 pages (illustrated). UK £11.95**
A crushingly honest account of his life as a junkie and a Ramone.
*"One of THE great rock and roll books...this is the true, awesome voice of The
Ramones"*. **Q magazine** *****
*"His story - knee deep in sex, drugs and rock and roll - is too incedent packed to
be anything less than gripping"*. **Mojo**
"A powerful work that is both confessional and exorcising" **Time Out.**

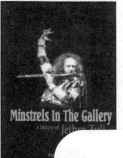

**Minstrels In The Gallery - A History of Jethro Tull by David Rees
ISBN: 0 946719 22 5   224 pages (illustrated) - UK £12.99**
At Last! To coincide with their 30th anniversary, a full history of one of the most
popular and inventive bands of the past three decades. Born out of the British
blues boom, Jethro Tull sped to worldwide success and superstardom - the band
were one of the biggest grossing acts of the seventies. With LPs like
Aqualung,Thick As A Brick and *Passion Play*, Anderson mutated from the wild-eyed
tramp through flute wielding minstrel to the country squire of rock n' roll.

...ll tale with zest and
...)JO

...n Prince. In this
...rior to the change
...e most productive
...ex-band members
...ost exciting black
...nes documentary

This store h...   ...title by
mail to a...   ...ct us.